University
WITHDRAWN FROM STOCK
& Systems
Inf   be returned immed-

MATERIALS FOR THE STUDY
OF BUSINESS

A Mathematical Reformulation of the General Theory of International Trade

THE UNIVERSITY OF CHICAGO PRESS
CHICAGO, ILLINOIS

—

THE BAKER & TAYLOR COMPANY
NEW YORK

THE CAMBRIDGE UNIVERSITY PRESS
LONDON

THE MARUZEN-KABUSHIKI-KAISHA
TOKYO, OSAKA, KYOTO, FUKUOKA, SENDAI

THE COMMERCIAL PRESS, LIMITED
SHANGHAI

A Mathematical Reformulation of the General Theory of International Trade

UNIVERSITY COLLEGE LIBRARY SWANSEA

By

THEODORE OTTE YNTEMA

Professor of Statistics, The School of Commerce and Administration
The University of Chicago

THE UNIVERSITY OF CHICAGO PRESS
CHICAGO ⸱ ILLINOIS

COPYRIGHT 1932 BY THE UNIVERSITY OF CHICAGO
ALL RIGHTS RESERVED. PUBLISHED MARCH 1932

COMPOSED AND PRINTED BY THE UNIVERSITY OF CHICAGO PRESS
CHICAGO, ILLINOIS, U.S.A.

TO
K.

PREFACE

The idea from which this dissertation grew was conceived under the stimulus of lectures on "International Economic Policies" delivered by Professor Jacob Viner. I am indebted to him for painstaking criticism, for constructive suggestions, for references—in fact, for most generous assistance at every turn. From Professor Henry Schultz I have received constant encouragement and, out of his wide knowledge of mathematical economics, technical aid which has been invaluable. My other major obligations are to Professors Frank Knight, Harold Hotelling, and John Canning for reading and commenting on the manuscript; to Professor F. W. Taussig and to the late Professor Allyn Young for instruction and inspiration; to Mr. Alexander Oppenheim for the solutions of Appendix I; and, not least, to a wife who "suffereth long and is kind." My debts to other teachers and friends are legion.

I am not so sanguine as to expect that I have avoided entirely errors of exposition or of theory. Responsibility for them is, of course, mine alone.

Chapter ii is the foundation upon which the three following chapters are separately based. If the reader prefers to omit the somewhat lengthy symbolic translations of chapter iii, he may proceed directly to chapters iv and v.

This monograph was originally submitted in partial fulfilment of the requirements for the doctorate in the University of Chicago, August, 1929. Except for the addition of section 4 in chapter v, no important revisions have been made in the original thesis.

Theodore O. Yntema

The University of Chicago
August 12, 1931

TABLE OF CONTENTS

CONTENTS

CHAPTER I

INTRODUCTION

The reformulation of the theory of international trade herein attempted does not constitute a system fundamentally different from the classical and neo-classical theory. Instead, it proceeds from well-known assumptions rather widely conceded to be useful approximations in many cases. By elementary methods of mathematical analysis the conclusions which follow from the classical premises are re-examined and extended.

The case for mathematical deduction is particularly strong in the theory of international trade. Within the general field of production and distribution the traditional one-thing-at-a-time method with its *ceteris paribus* assumption typically yields useful approximations, since the repercussions of a given change are often negligible, or at least insufficient to alter the sign of the direct result. On the other hand, the simultaneous equation analysis—much as it may contribute to an appreciation of the assumptions implicit in a simplified technique—suffers as a method of direct approach from the severe practical limitation of complexity, since it introduces innumerable elements but little related to the immediate phenomenon. The respective merits of these procedures, however, are quite different when applied to the theory of international trade. Here the classical method has been particularly awkward, and the field has often been designated as the most difficult and perplexing in economics. For the validity of the *ceteris paribus* assumption is doubtful if the problem is one related to loans, indemnities, duties, bounties, etc. (not restricted to a very small portion of the imports or the exports), since the repercussions of changes in price levels and exchange rates on the interrelations of supply and demand are of primary importance. The term "reciprocal demand" nicely epitomizes the vagueness of classical theory in this realm. But these conditions afford the best opportunity for mathematical analysis. A relatively small number of variables, closely interdependent, but—as a useful first approximation—independent of *repercussions* from the multitude of factors in the domestic price system, offers the chance to use the *ceteris paribus* assumption relative to the latter and the method of simultaneous equations in analyzing relations between the former.

The group of closely related variables to be dealt with in international trade theory are those of prices and quantities of the commodities demanded and supplied. The relations of this group to substitute domestic commodities might also be recognized, and it would be possible to include a wider and wider range of variables until the whole price system of each country were involved in the adjustment of trade balances. For a complete theory this would be necessary. But the equations would then be so numerous and complicated as to afford nothing more than an indication of the type of relations existing at equilibrium. Utilizing more restricted assumptions, we shall be able to derive and extend the principal propositions in the pure theory of international trade.

It is believed that the contributions to be found in these pages consist in (1) a more accurate definition of assumptions; (2) a simpler and more elegant statement of equilibrium conditions; (3) a technique for analyzing—subject to the assumptions made— the effects of a disturbance in conditions of demand or supply or in trade balances; (4) a method for generalizing many of these conclusions to any number of commodities and countries; and (5), perhaps, a basis for a statistical approach to some problems in international prices.

CHAPTER II

THE GENERAL EQUATIONS DESCRIBING EQUILIBRIUM

1. PREVIEW OF THE CHAPTER

At the risk of oversimplification and later repetition we shall preface this chapter with a general statement of procedure. It is hoped that such a preview may suggest how the preliminary assumptions and definitions will be synthesized into a description of equilibrium.

International trade, or, as it is often termed, interregional trade, is in the pure case distinguished from intranational or intraregional trade by immobility of the productive agents between the countries or regions.[1] Only exchange of *products* takes place between the countries. Actually this sharp contrast of sufficient mobility of the factors for competition and equalization of price within the respective regions with complete immobility between regions does not exist. In this study we shall confine ourselves to the simplified, ideal case.

In most instances the changes in the prices of imported or exported commodities attributable to disturbances in the conditions of trade may, for our purposes, be resolved into two components: (*a*) shifts of all the demand and supply schedules of a country up or down by a ratio which is constant for every point on any schedule; (*b*) movements of the equilibrium price points along the schedules with changes in quantities demanded or supplied. The shifts of class (*a*) are monetary in character, resulting from a generally distributed increase or decrease in the means of payment in cir-

---

[1] We shall hereafter use the term "country" as indicative of a region within which the productive factors are in competition, but beyond the limits of which they cannot move.

culation. If we could abstract from them, it would be possible, for some arbitrarily assumed monetary conditions, to define the ordinary price-quantity functions of demand and supply. Shifts which are peculiar to specific schedules are not included under either (a) or (b) but constitute a separate class.

There are two well-known, fundamental characteristics of exchange between individuals, trading bodies, or countries, which are readily translated into equations. At equilibrium price the quantity of a commodity demanded is equal to the quantity supplied. Or, in special form for our use: at a price which is the same in all countries (neglecting transportation costs, duties, etc.) the total quantities of a commodity imported are equal to the total quantities exported. This is true of, and yields an equation for, each commodity. The second condition is this: for each trading body or country the total value of what is bought is equal to the total value of what is sold, allowance being made for loans, deferred payments, gifts, etc. This corresponds to the balance of international debits and credits and reduces in the simplest case to the equality of the value of exports and imports. From this relation one equation is obtained for each country. These two sets of equations, together with those necessary to define the functions and assert the equality of international prices, are adequate for a description of equilibrium.

We may now pass to a more detailed analysis of the problem.

2. STATEMENT OF ASSUMPTIONS

Pursuing the classical method of abstracting from complicating factors, we shall first write the equations describing equilibrium in international trade for a very simple case. The list of assumptions cited below (an inclusion not strictly in the classical tradition) is not complete in detail; many of the assumptions are of blanket character covering numerous subordinate points.

Assumption 1: Invisible items, i.e., non-commodity items, such as loans, indemnities, duties, etc., do not enter into trade balances.

Assumption 2: Physical, financial, or time barriers to trade, such as embargoes, transportation costs, duties, etc., do not exist.

Assumption 3: Competition brings about the equality of the values of every internationally traded commodity in all exporting and importing countries in terms of gold or in terms of any other traded commodity.

Assumption 4: Definite demand and supply schedules for each commodity are given. A demand schedule allows the whole quantity of a commodity taken by domestic buyers to be stated as a function of the price of the commodity, provided that abstraction is made from other influences, including *monetary* changes. A supply schedule permits the quantity of a commodity offered for sale by the whole group of domestic vendors to be expressed as a function of its price—again abstracting from all other effects on the price. These are the ordinary domestic demand and supply schedules, defined for some constant set of monetary conditions.[1]

The assumption of such schedules is indeed significant, since it implies, *inter alia:*

a) There is a definite functional relationship between price and quantity with respect to commodities supplied and demanded. In particular the price is a single-valued function of the quantity.

b) Shifts and migration of the factors of production resulting from changes in international trade are neglected.

c) No internationally traded commodity has any rival or complementary commodity.

Assumption 5: Adjustment in international trade to equilibrium conditions is achieved through monetary mechanisms which elevate the demand and supply schedules of some countries and lower the schedules of other countries, or alter the exchange values of the currencies of the various countries, or operate in both these

---

[1] Constant monetary conditions are such as would keep the prices of purely domestic commodities (i.e., commodities not traded internationally) constant. Although the prices of exported and imported commodities might vary under these conditions with variations in the quantities of imports or exports, their demand and supply schedules would remain unchanged.

ways concurrently. If a monetary change raises or depresses the schedules in a country, *all* the schedules of that country are raised or depressed *throughout* by the same ratio.

Assumption 6: Only such *original* disturbing influences occur as are directly recognized in the analysis.

Of these assumptions, the first three are obviously not true to the facts and, as we shall see, can be somewhat modified to accord better with actual conditions. Assumption 4 can be relaxed to allow rival and complementary relations between commodities, but the analysis then becomes much more complicated. It has not been feasible to do this except in the general equations. The fifth assumption is essential to a simple algebraic description of equilibrium and cannot readily be modified without introducing other arbitrary elements. It can, however, be abandoned, as in chapter v, when we are seeking only the *signs* of the changes in the variables resulting from a disturbance to equilibrium.

Attention should be directed to the assumption of price-quantity functions—particularly supply functions—since they are a considerable simplification of actual conditions. Even though we specify whether we are considering short- or long-run adjustments, we should recognize the fact that short- and long-run adjustments do not occur independently of each other. But we follow what we believe to be a useful abstraction in assuming supply and demand curves as elements of our problem. There is this consideration in support of such procedure, that if we know only whether the demand curves be inelastic or elastic and whether the supply curves' slopes be positive or negative, we can, in some instances, formulate generalizations regarding the sign of the change in the prices of the commodities and the quantities imported and exported.

The implications of the fifth assumption should not be overlooked. It excludes other mechanisms which aid in establishing equilibrium, such as partial movements of the factors of production and changes in the amounts of invisible items which minimize short-run oscillations in exchange rates and price levels. Furthermore,[1] the mechanism described in this assumption is based on a much simplified theory of money and prices. Current formulations of monetary theory show that in the expansion or contraction of credit and currency, demand and supply schedules do not shift by a uniform ratio. Movements in price levels are phenomena with important dynamic characteristics which cannot be described in static terms. Our procedure is not, however, wholly unwarranted. For the tendency of such dynamic changes is toward the conditions indicated by our uniform shifts of schedules. The degree of accuracy of our assumption depends upon the length of period of adjustment considered and the uniformity and simultaneity with which expansion and contraction of credit affect the income streams of primary importance in determining the prices of imports and exports.

From assumptions 1 and 2 and the implicit assumption that what is bought is paid for immediately, it follows that the total value of exports from each country must equal the total value of imports into that country for any given period. Further, for any period, the total quantity of imports of a commodity into all countries must equal the total quantity of exports of the commodity from all countries. These two well-known generalizations, coupled with the fifth assumption regarding the monetary shifts in demand and supply schedules, afford the basis for the equations of equilibrium in international trade.

3. DEFINITION OF SYMBOLS

Let there be countries 1 to m engaged in international trade, identified by a *first* subscript (or first after a comma, if one appears in the subscripts) to any variable or function, and commodities 1 to n, identified by a *second* subscript (or second after a comma).[2]

---

[1] The conclusions of chapter v are not, for the most part, subject to the limitations cited in the rest of this paragraph.

[2] After much consideration it seemed best to abandon the scheme of symbols ordinarily used by the Lausanne mathematical school of economists and adopt a

In some preliminary cases and in a few instances later it is necessary to distinguish the price, quantity, function, or elasticity of a demand curve from that of a supply curve. This is done by using a subscript d or s, then a comma, and after the comma the country and commodity subscripts. Let x_{pk} be the quantity[1] of commodity k exported from (if x is positive) or imported into (if x is negative)[2] country p. Let y_{pk} be the price which the kth commodity would have in the pth country under some *constant* monetary conditions arbitrarily assumed, so that all demand and supply schedules could be defined at fixed heights for these conditions. Let $q_{d,pk}$ be the quantity of the kth commodity taken in the pth country, and similarly let $q_{s,pk}$ be the quantity supplied.

---

system of double-subscript notation. Among the reasons for this decision the following are the most weighty:

a) Some device for identifying many different variables and functions with the particular commodity and country is necessary. The subscript notation does this most conveniently.

b) The double-subscript system conforms to the ordinary mathematical notation and greatly facilitates the handling of the determinants in chapter v and Appendix I.

c) It is often useful to be able to write a general term or a general equation typifying a large group of such terms and equations. For this the general subscripts are a distinct advantage.

d) Subscripts, particularly numerical subscripts, facilitate the writing of summations in abbreviated form.

e) The use of subscripts avoids the introduction of an excessive number of symbols.

For illustration of the use of double-subscript notation in analogous circumstances, see A. L. Bowley, *Mathematical Groundwork of Economics*, pp. 5 ff., and V. Pareto, "Teoria Matematica dei Cambi Forestieri," *Giornale degli Economisti*, VIII (1894), 143 ff.

[1] All quantities demanded or supplied, or imported or exported, are really rates, i.e., quantities per unit of time.

[2] This use of a positive sign for exports and a negative sign for imports leads to a determinant in chapter v in which all the elements are positive rather than negative. The distinction between positively and negatively sloped supply curves, which is important, would also be confused by the use of negative signs for exports. In spite of the fact that our convention is at variance with ordinary usage, it seemed advisable to adopt it.

Between these quantities and the quantity exported $(+)$ or imported $(-)$ there is the obvious relation:

$$q_{s,pk} - q_{d,pk} = x_{pk} .\tag{1}$$

Now our assumptions permit us to express the quantity taken (or supplied) as a function of the price on a fixed-height schedule.

$$q_{s,pk} = \psi_{s,pk}(y_{pk}) .\tag{2}$$

$$q_{d,pk} = \psi_{d,pk}(y_{pk}) .\tag{3}$$

Consequently the quantity exported or imported may be defined (*except for imports of a commodity produced under decreasing costs*)[1] as

$$x_{pk} = q_{s,pk} - q_{d,pk} = \psi_{s,pk}(y_{pk}) - \psi_{d,pk}(y_{pk})\tag{4}$$

or simply,

$$x_{pk} = f_{pk}(y_{pk}) .\tag{5}$$

Conversely, of course, y may be expressed as a function of x:

$$y_{pk} = \phi_{pk}(x_{pk}) .\tag{6}$$

Now y_{pk} has been defined and related to x_{pk} for some assumed, *constant* monetary conditions. But it is through *changes* in monetary conditions that adjustments in international trade are effected. Such changes, according to our assumptions, shift all the de-

[1] This definition is appropriate if the supply curve is positively sloped and also for *exports* of a commodity whose curve of equation (2) is negatively sloped. For *imports* of a commodity whose supply in the importing country would be characterized by a negatively sloped curve this relation is not correct. For such imports the proper function is

$$x_{pk} = -\psi_{d,pk}(y_{pk}) .\tag{4a}$$

The function $f_{pk}(y_{pk})$ in equation (5) is under these conditions defined by (4a) instead of (4). A full explanation of this matter is given in chapter iv, where the problem can be dealt with more conveniently by graphic illustrations.

mand and supply schedules of a country upward or downward by some ratio which is the same for all commodities. Let us designate by Y_{pk} the *actual* money price of the kth commodity in the pth country. Then if r_p be the ratio of the height of any schedule in country p under existing conditions to the height of the same schedule under the assumed conditions for which its y_{pk} was defined and related to x_{pk}, we have

$$r_p = \frac{Y_{pk}}{y_{pk}} . \tag{7}$$

Thus, for example, if all the schedules in country p had risen by 25 per cent above the status under which y_{pk} was defined,

$$r_p = 1.25 = \frac{Y_{pk}}{y_{pk}} . \tag{8}$$

For the exchange rate, i.e., the number of units of currency of country p obtainable for one unit of the currency of country 1, let us use the symbol $c_{\frac{1}{p}}$. Since the prices of internationally traded commodities are the same in both countries when allowance is made for the exchange rate, it follows that

$$c_{\frac{1}{p}} Y_{1k} = Y_{pk} . \tag{9}$$

Let us next consider the relations between the heights of the schedules in countries 1 and p and the exchange rate. If the number of units of currency in country 1 were twice what it is, the heights of all the schedules would be doubled. On the other hand, the number of units of currency of country p obtainable for a unit of the currency of country 1 would be halved. Such a phenomenon we shall term a *compensated* monetary change, i.e., a shift in the ratio of the two price levels compensated by a reverse shift in the exchange rate, or, from the other point of view, a shift in the exchange rate compensated by a reverse shift in the ratio of the two price levels. Such compensated monetary changes, which form the basis for the purchasing power parity theory, leave the net value of the expression $\frac{r_1}{r_p} c_{\frac{1}{p}}$ unchanged, since a proportional increase or decrease in $\frac{r_1}{r_p}$ is balanced by the same proportional decrease or increase in $c_{\frac{1}{p}}$. Any net change in $\left(\frac{r_1}{r_p} c_{\frac{1}{p}}\right)$ we shall call an *uncompensated* monetary change, and the expression $\left(\frac{r_1}{r_p} c_{\frac{1}{p}}\right)$ we shall designate by the symbol $z_{\frac{1}{p}}$, which we shall term the *net monetary factor*.

$$z_{\frac{1}{p}} = \frac{r_1}{r_p} c_{\frac{1}{p}}. \tag{10}$$

Obviously, $z_{\frac{1}{p}}$ varies directly with the ratio of the height of country 1's schedules to the height of country p's schedules and also directly with the exchange rate. Consequently, if the exchange rate $c_{\frac{1}{p}}$ is constant, the net monetary factor $z_{\frac{1}{p}}$ varies directly with the ratio of the heights of the schedules in the two countries, $\frac{r_1}{r_p}$. But if this ratio is constant, the net monetary factor $z_{\frac{1}{p}}$ is directly proportional to $c_{\frac{1}{p}}$, the exchange rate.

By substitution in (10) from (7) we get

$$z_{\frac{1}{p}} = \frac{r_1}{r_p} c_{\frac{1}{p}} = \frac{\dfrac{Y_{1k}}{y_{1k}}}{\dfrac{Y_{pk}}{y_{pk}}} c_{\frac{1}{p}} = \frac{y_{pk}}{y_{1k}} \frac{Y_{1k}}{Y_{pk}} c_{\frac{1}{p}}. \tag{11}$$

But by (9) we have

$$\frac{Y_{1k}}{Y_{pk}} c_{\frac{1}{p}} = 1. \tag{12}$$

Whence

$$z_{\mathrm{I}} = \frac{y_{pk}}{y_{\mathrm{I}k}} \quad \text{or} \quad y_{pk} = z_{\mathrm{I}} y_{\mathrm{I}k} \,. \tag{13}$$

On the significance of this relation two observations should be made. First, corresponding to the equivalence of money prices of internationally traded commodities in two countries (when allowance is made for the exchange rate), we have here the proposition that the ratio $\frac{y_{pk}}{y_{\mathrm{I}k}}$ is the same for all traded commodities. Second, it is clear that a change in the net monetary factor z_{I} signifies that there has been a real or uncompensated shift in the relation of the schedules in country 1 to those in country p. These uncompensated or real shifts in the heights of the schedules or in the exchange rates afford the basis for adjustments in international trade necessitated by changes in conditions of demand and supply, indemnities, duties, etc.—i.e., such disturbances as are not of a purely monetary character involving only the general heights of the schedules and the exchange rates.

4. THE EQUILIBRIUM EQUATIONS

Having defined all the necessary symbols, we are equipped to describe the characteristics of equilibrium in international trade The two fundamental conditions of equilibrium are, for our simplest case, the equality of the *values* of the imports and the exports for *each country*, and the equality of the *quantities* of the exports and the imports of each *commodity* for all countries combined. The equations of Sets I and II below exhibit these two conditions respectively. Sets III, IV, and V are auxiliary equations stating the interrelations of the quantities and the prices and the variations in the heights of the schedules, as set forth in the preceding paragraphs. The demonstration of the equality of the number of equations and unknowns, which is necessary for a determinate solution, may best be deferred to a later point in the discussion.

Set I.—Each equation states that the sum of the values of goods imported ($-$) plus the sum of the values of goods exported ($+$) is zero for each country. We have, thus, m equations, one for each country, of the type, for the pth country,

$$x_{p1}Y_{p1}+x_{p2}Y_{p2}+x_{p3}Y_{p3}+\cdots\cdots+x_{pn}Y_{pn}=0 , \qquad (14)$$

or, in summation form,

$$\sum_{i=1}^{i=n} x_{pi}Y_{pi}=0 .$$

Set II.—For each commodity the sum of the quantities exported ($+$) from all countries plus the sum of the quantities imported ($-$) into all countries must be zero. There are n such equations, one for each commodity, of the type, for the kth commodity,

$$x_{1k}+x_{2k}+x_{3k}+\cdots\cdots+x_{mk}=0 , \qquad (15)$$

or, in summation form,

$$\sum_{i=1}^{i=m} x_{ik}=0 .$$

Set III.—Rewriting (7),

$$Y_{pk}=r_p y_{pk} . \qquad (16)$$

There is one such equation for each of the n commodities in each of the m countries, mn equations in all. r_p is the same for every commodity in a country.

Set IV.—From (5) we obtain mn equations, one for each commodity in each country,

$$x_{pk}=f_{pk}(y_{pk}) . \qquad (17)$$

Set V.—From (13)[1]

$$y_{pk} = z_{\underset{p}{1}} y_{1k} \; . \tag{18}$$

There are n such equations (one for each commodity) for each of $(m-1)$ countries, or $n(m-1)$ in all. For country 1, $z_{\underset{1}{1}}$ is unity and the equation becomes a simple identity.

By substituting in the equations of Sets I and II the expressions given by Sets III, IV, and V, we can eliminate the latter sets and obtain $(m+n)$ equations involving only the y_{1k}'s and the $z_{\underset{p}{1}}$'s.

We may first substitute from Set V in Set III and Set IV. (The Roman numerals in brackets specify the sets of equations from which substitution has been made.)

Set III (V).

$$Y_{pk} = r_p z_{\underset{p}{1}} y_{1k} \; . \tag{19}$$

Set IV (V).

$$x_{pk} = f_{pk}(z_{\underset{p}{1}} y_{1k}) \; . \tag{20}$$

We then substitute these expressions for Y_{pk} and x_{pk} in Set I, obtaining

$$r_p z_{\underset{p}{1}} y_{11} f_{p1}(z_{\underset{p}{1}} y_{11}) + r_p z_{\underset{p}{1}} y_{12} f_{p2}(z_{\underset{p}{1}} y_{12}) + \cdots + r_p z_{\underset{p}{1}} y_{1n} f_{pn}(z_{\underset{p}{1}} y_{1n}) = 0 \; , \tag{21}$$

or

$$\sum_{i=1}^{i=n} r_p z_{\underset{p}{1}} y_{1i} f_{pi}(z_{\underset{p}{1}} y_{1i}) = 0 \; .$$

---

[1] If commodity k is not an internationally traded commodity for country 1, there is no $y_{pk} = z_{\underset{p}{1}} y_{1k}$ relation to be used in substituting for y_{pk}. But the relation of y_{pk} to y_{gk} (for the gth country) may be used instead by virtue of (26):

$$y_{pk} = \frac{z_{\underset{p}{1}}}{z_{\underset{g}{1}}} y_{gk} \; . \tag{18a}$$

This relation, it should be noticed, does not introduce any additional variables.

From this r_p may be canceled out, giving Set I (III, IV, V):

$$\sum_{i=1}^{i=n} z_{\underset{p}{1}} y_{1i} f_{pi}(z_{\underset{p}{1}} y_{1i}) = 0 . \qquad (22)$$

Further, if we wish, the $z_{\underset{p}{1}}$ may be canceled, since it is common to all the commodities.

Set I' (III, IV, V).

$$\sum_{i=1}^{i=n} y_{1i} f_{pi}(z_{\underset{p}{1}} y_{1i}) = 0 . \qquad (23)$$

By substitution in Set II from Set IV (V), we obtain Set II (IV, V):

$$f_{1k}(y_{1k}) + f_{2k}(z_{\underset{2}{1}} y_{1k}) + f_{3k}(z_{\underset{3}{1}} y_{1k}) + \dots + f_{mk}(z_{\underset{m}{1}} y_{1k}) = 0 , \qquad (24)$$

or, since $z_{\underset{1}{1}}$ is unity,

$$\sum_{i=1}^{i=m} f_{ik}(z_{\underset{i}{1}} y_{1k}) = 0 .$$

Together, Sets I (III, IV, V), (22), and II (IV, V), (24), contain $(m+n)$ equations. They involve n unknowns, y_{1k}, and $(m-1)$ unknowns, $z_{\underset{p}{1}}$, together $(m+n-1)$ unknowns. But one of the equations can be obtained from the other $(m+n-1)$ by straightforward substitution, so that there are the same number of independent equations as unknowns.[1]

The final two sets of equations, Set I' (III, IV, V), i.e., (23), and Set II (IV, V), (24), may be written in a simple rectangular for-

[1] This can be most easily seen by reference to equations (25). Suppose, for example, that the *equation* in the first row was not given. For each term in the first row its equivalent, which is the negative sum of the other terms in its vertical column, may be substituted. But the sum of all such terms is zero. Therefore the sum of the terms in the first row is zero.

mation, equations of the former set reading from left to right and equations of the latter set, with a factor y_{1k} inserted throughout, reading from top to bottom.

$$y_{11}f_{11}(y_{11}) \; +y_{12}f_{12}(y_{12}) \; +\cdots +y_{1n}f_{1n}(y_{1n}) \; =0$$

$$+ \qquad\qquad + \qquad\qquad\qquad +$$

$$y_{11}f_{21}(z_1 y_{11})+y_{12}f_{22}(z_1 y_{12})+\cdots +y_{1n}f_{2n}(z_1 y_{1n})=0$$
$$\quad\;\; 2 \qquad\qquad\;\; 2 \qquad\qquad\qquad\;\; 2$$

$$+ \qquad\qquad + \qquad\qquad\qquad +$$

$$y_{11}f_{31}(z_1 y_{11})+y_{12}f_{32}(z_1 y_{12})+\cdots +y_{1n}f_{3n}(z_1 y_{1n})=0 \qquad (25)$$
$$\quad\;\; 3 \qquad\qquad\;\; 3 \qquad\qquad\qquad\;\; 3$$

$$+ \qquad\qquad + \qquad\qquad\qquad +$$
$$\cdot \qquad\qquad \cdot \qquad\qquad\qquad \cdot$$
$$\cdot \qquad\qquad \cdot \qquad\qquad\qquad \cdot \qquad \cdot$$
$$\cdot \qquad\qquad \cdot \qquad\qquad\qquad \cdot$$
$$\cdot \qquad\qquad \cdot \qquad\qquad\qquad \cdot$$
$$+ \qquad\qquad + \qquad\qquad\qquad +$$

$$y_{11}f_{m1}(z_1 y_{11})+y_{12}f_{m2}(z_1 y_{12})+\cdots +y_{1n}f_{mn}(z_1 y_{1n})=0$$
$$\quad\;\; m \qquad\qquad\;\; m \qquad\qquad\qquad\;\; m$$

$$\| \qquad\qquad \| \qquad\quad \cdots \qquad \|$$
$$0 \qquad\qquad 0 \qquad\qquad\qquad 0$$

These horizontal equations, it will be remembered, are derived from the fact that the sum of values of imports $(-)$ and values of exports $(+)$ equals zero for each country. And the vertical equations indicate that the sum of the quantities of a commodity imported $(-)$ into all countries and the quantities exported $(+)$ from all countries is zero.

From the equations of Sets I (III, IV, V) and II (IV, V), as given in (22) and (24) or in (25), the y_{1k}'s (the prices on fixed-height schedules of all the commodities for country 1) and the z_1's (all the net monetary factors) are determinable. Through the equations of Set V, (18), all the y_{pk}'s (the prices on the fixed-height schedules of all the commodities in *all* the countries) are then calculable; and from them, by means of the equations of Set

IV, (17), all the x_{pk}'s (the quantities of imports and exports for all commodities and all respective countries). The actual money prices, Y_{pk}, which appear in Set III, (16), cannot be determined since we do not have the means of ascertaining the r_p values. These ratios, r_p, establish the absolute heights of the actual demand and supply schedules in existing money units for the various countries. Since equilibrium is dependent, not on the absolute heights, but on the *relative* heights of the schedules in the respective countries and on the exchange rates, it is to be expected that the ratios, r_p, are not involved in the solution. They can be ascertained only by knowledge of the factors which fix the absolute heights of price levels throughout the world.

5. THE NET MONETARY FACTOR

The net monetary factor $\dfrac{z_1}{p}$ which is the key to our simultaneous equation description of equilibrium, was by (10) defined as equal to $\left(\dfrac{r_1}{r_p} \dfrac{c_1}{p} \right)$. Now, if the exchange values of all currencies—or of the currencies of those particular countries in which we are interested—were known and were constant, i.e., if the $\dfrac{c_1}{p}$'s were known constants (a condition approximated when the countries are on the gold standard), all the ratios between the r_p's could evidently be ascertained. Further, if from data outside those which have been assumed, any r_p were known, then the other r_p's would be calculable. Changes in the ratio $\dfrac{r_1}{r_p}$ would be approximately the same, if $\dfrac{c_1}{p}$ were constant, as changes in the ratio of the height of the internal or domestic price level of country 1 relative to that of country p.

On the other hand, if the r_p's in question were constant, i.e., if the *actual* schedules in these countries were to remain throughout at fixed heights, a case approximated when the internal price

levels are constant, the net monetary factor $\frac{z_i}{p}$ would be proportional to the exchange rate $\frac{c_i}{p}$, which represents the number of
units of currency of country p which have a purchasing power of
any internationally traded commodity equal to that of one unit of
the currency of country i. In the special case in which the r_p's
were all unity, the net monetary factor $\frac{z_i}{p}$ would be identical with
the exchange rate $\frac{c_i}{p}$.

Neither of the special cases discussed in the two preceding
paragraphs will necessarily exist, and it is quite possible that
variations in the net monetary factor $\frac{z_i}{p}$ will be the result of con-
current variations in the relative heights of the price levels and
in the exchange rate, i.e., in both $\frac{r_i}{r_p}$ and $\frac{c_i}{p}$. It is hardly necessary
to remark that, if it is desired, a net monetary factor, $\frac{z_g}{p}$, relating
country g to country p could be calculated from the relation,

$$z_{\frac{g}{p}} = \frac{r_g}{r_p} c_{\frac{g}{p}} = \frac{z_{\frac{i}{p}}}{z_{\frac{i}{g}}}. \tag{26}$$

6. LIMITATIONS OF THE PURCHASING POWER PARITY THEORY

The foregoing exposition may throw some light on the doctrine
of purchasing power parity in its simpler forms. According to
this doctrine, the exchange ratio of the currencies of two countries
is inversely proportional to the ratio of their domestic price levels.
Assuming no disturbances to originate except those which we
specifically recognize, $\frac{r_i}{r_p}$ is proportional to the ratio between the
heights of the two price levels and $\frac{c_i}{p}$ is the exchange ratio of the
currencies. Consequently, the doctrine requires that

$$\frac{r_1}{r_p} = K \frac{1}{\dfrac{c_1}{p}}, \tag{27}$$

in which K is some constant, and also therefore that

$$\frac{z_1}{p} = K . \tag{28}$$

But it is variations in this net monetary factor, $\frac{z_1}{p}$, which are all important in explaining the adjustments necessitated by non-monetary changes, such as shifts in demand, indemnities, loans, duties, etc. Because it requires implicitly that the net monetary factor be a constant, the purchasing power parity theory is completely estopped from coping with such phenomena and is compelled to regard them as disturbing factors for which it cannot account. It can deal adequately only with those changes of a purely monetary origin and character in which price levels and exchange rates require appropriate adjustment *to each other*, i.e., in which only a "compensated monetary change" occurs.

7. THE TERMS OF TRADE IN RESOURCES COSTS

Thus far we have deliberately refrained from introducing relative resources costs or terms of trade as measured in resources. It seemed preferable to develop our formulation first by discussing more realistic price phenomena than to encumber it with the perplexities of real costs. But the basis for the analysis of many of these issues has been provided by our formulation—in some ways better perhaps than if the problem had been approached directly. $\frac{z_1}{p}$ has been named the net monetary factor; subject to certain restrictions, it might have been called an "index" of the resources terms of trade, i.e., an index of the ratio of the quantity of resources of country p to the quantity of resources of country 1, necessary in the respective countries to yield products of equal exchange value. *If y_{pk} and y_{1k} may be assumed proportional to the*

*resources costs of producing a unit of commodity k in the respective
countries*, $z_{\underline{1}\atop p}$, which is by (13) equal to the ratio of y_{pk} to y_{1k},
would be such an index. The definition may be made more general by requiring only that under constant monetary conditions a unit of money in country 1 (and similarly for country p) shall be able to purchase a constant quantity of productive resources. It is then unnecessary that the commodity be produced in both countries. This index of the terms of trade avoids some of the difficulties encountered in the usual exposition of the theory. In the first place, there is absolutely no necessity that the units of productive resources in countries 1 and p be identical. Secondly, the composition of a unit of productive resources may be allowed to vary; substitution of one resource for another in the unit is made at the current rate of exchange (value) between resources. No difficulty arises so long as it may be assumed that under constant monetary conditions for a country one money unit will always purchase the same quantity of any factor of production, or, if any variation in this quantity occurs, that it is proportionately the same for all productive factors. When changes in the relative prices of the productive factors must be considered, the effects of *small* alterations in the composition of the unit of productive resources could be *approximated* by the use of index numbers.[1]

The resources terms of trade is not equivalent to the commodity terms of trade, sometimes called the "barter" or "net barter" terms of trade. This latter is the ratio of a quantity of representative exports to a quantity of representative imports of equal value, and its variations are conveniently measured by

---

[1] The index of the resources terms of trade might be regarded also as an index of the terms of trade in marginal sacrifice or real costs, if for each individual the prices of the various productive services or resources which he provided or sold were proportional to his marginal disutility of supplying them. (The forgoing of the return from an alternative use is here considered as a sacrifice, e.g., in the case of land.) This proportionality of the prices of factors of production to the sacrifice costs of supplying them really underlies and justifies the substitution of one resource for another in a composite unit of resources.

dividing an index of the price of imports by an index of the price of exports. If country 1 imported only a single commodity, 1, and exported only a single commodity, 2, an index of the commodity or barter terms of trade would be given by $\dfrac{Y_{11}}{Y_{12}}$, or its equivalent, $\dfrac{y_{11}}{y_{12}}$. Now y_{12} would generally be an index of the resources cost of a unit of exports from country 1. But y_{p1}, which would generally be an index of the resources cost to the exporting country, p, of a unit of commodity 1 imported by country 1, is neither equal nor proportional to y_{11}, but is equal to y_{11} multiplied by the variable $z_{\frac{1}{p}}$. Consequently, it is not legitimate to assume that the commodity or barter terms of trade is a reliable index of the resources terms of trade. The argument may be put in more general terms. Disturbances to international equilibrium cause the command of (convertible) money over resources in the various countries to undergo changes which are not uniform as regards the different countries. Hence the ratios of the money prices of the exports of the different countries cannot serve as indexes of the ratios of their resources costs.

8. AN ALTERNATIVE SET OF EQUILIBRIUM EQUATIONS

There are other ways in which the equilibrium equations may be combined and simplified. We may utilize Sets I, II, III, and V, numbered (14), (15), (16), and (18), respectively, and add to these, in place of Set IV, (17), a Set VI from (6), of the type,

$$y_{pk} = \phi_{pk}(x_{pk}) . \tag{29}$$

Since there is one such equation for each commodity in each country, there are mn equations in the set. From Set VI substitution can be made in Set III, (16), and in Set V, (18), yielding Sets III (VI) and V (VI):

$$Y_{pk} = r_p \phi_{pk}(x_{pk}) . \tag{30}$$

$$\phi_{pk}(x_{pk}) = z_{\frac{1}{p}} \phi_{1k}(x_{1k}) . \tag{31}$$

Substituting in Set I, (14), from Set III (VI), (30), and canceling out the r_p, we get Set I (III, VI):

$$x_{p1}\phi_{p1}(x_{p1}) + x_{p2}\phi_{p2}(x_{p2}) + x_{p3}\phi_{p3}(x_{p3}) + \cdots + x_{pn}\phi_{pn}(x_{pn}) = 0 , \quad (32)$$

or in the summed form,

$$\sum_{i=1}^{i=n} x_{pi}\phi_{pi}(x_{pi}) = 0 .$$

Now Sets I (III, VI), (32), and V (VI), (31), together with Set II, (15), contain the following number of unknowns:

x_{pk}, one for each commodity in each country,......mn
$z_{\frac{1}{p}}$, one for each country except 1,.. ....$m-1$

Total number of unknowns................$mn+m-1$

The number of equations in these sets is as follows:

Set I (III, VI), (32) ....m
Set II, (15)...................................n
Set V (VI), (31)............................$n(m-1)$

Total number of equations ....$mn+m$

We have, therefore, as before, one more equation than unknowns. But any one of the equations of the Sets I (III, VI), (32), and II, (15), can be obtained from the other $(m+n-1)$ by direct substitution. Hence there are but $(mn+m-1)$ independent equations and the solution is, prima facie, determinate.

Because of the much larger number of unknowns left when the equations are reduced in this latter way, it is usually more convenient to deal with the forms first derived, Sets I (III, IV, V), (22), and II (IV, V), (24).

9. DETERMINATION OF ABSOLUTE MONEY PRICES

Although for many problems the relative prices in each country will suffice, it is sometimes desirable to know how the absolute prices are determined.

If all the countries in the system were on (stable) inconvertible paper currencies, the heights of the actual money demand and supply schedules, and hence the r_p's, would be known. It would, as a matter of fact, be convenient to assume for the definition of the y_{pk}'s the constant monetary conditions actually in existence, so that all the r_p's would be equal to unity. With the r_p's known, the actual money prices, Y_{pk}, would be ascertainable from the fixed-height schedule prices, y_{pk}.

$$Y_{pk} = r_p y_{pk} . \qquad (33)$$

Under inconvertible paper currencies gold would have a variable money price and fixed-height schedules like those of any other commodity. Unless the equations of this chapter are modified as indicated in the following paragraphs, they are applicable to gold only if all countries have inconvertible currencies.

The essence of the gold standard and convertibility of the currency is a fixed money price for gold (fixed at least within narrow limits). If gold be the gth commodity, this simply means that in any gold-standard country p the price Y_{pg} is a known constant. The fixed-height schedule price of gold is the variable y_{pg}, equal to $\dfrac{Y_{pg}}{r_p}$. If for the y_{pg} of each gold-standard country we substitute in our equations $\dfrac{Y_{pg}}{r_p}$, we shall be replacing each variable y_{pg} by an expression involving a variable r_p. The number of unknowns will therefore remain unchanged, and the system of equations will remain determinate. Since the r_p and the y_{pk}'s for all the commodities are simultaneously determined by the solution of the equations, the actual money prices, Y_{pk}, are at once calculable from (33). By means of equation (10) any r_p for a gold-standard country can be obtained if r_1 is known, since $\frac{c_1}{p}$ is a constant between gold-standard countries. The actual money prices in any gold-standard country could be ascertained then by use of (33), or directly by (9).

For gold-standard countries the demand function for gold requires a word of interpretation. $q_{d,pq}$ should be taken for the pth country as the quantity of gold per unit of time consumed in the arts plus the quantity necessary to make good the depletion of the monetary stock due to loss and wear. Thus, at equilibrium, the quantity of gold supplied throughout the world would be equal to the quantity demanded in the arts plus the quantity to replace the depletion of the monetary stock of the metal.

The total monetary gold stock and its distribution among the various countries might be determined as follows. Let the gold-standard countries, numbered 1 to m', possess a total stock of gold represented by the *unknown* W, expressed in units of the currency of country 1. Let the total money payments per unit of time at fixed-height schedule prices in the respective countries be the known constants $v_1, v_2, \ldots v_{m'}$. Then the total money payments at actual prices would be $r_1v_1, r_2v_2, \ldots r_mv_{m'}$. Let the ratio of gold stock to money payments for each country be $u_1, u_2, \ldots u_{m'}$, which are also regarded as constants. Then we get the equation:

$$r_1v_1u_1 + \frac{r_2v_2u_2}{c_{\frac{1}{2}}} + \frac{r_3v_3u_3}{c_{\frac{1}{3}}} + \cdots + \frac{r_{m'}v_{m'}u_{m'}}{c_{\frac{1}{m'}}} = W \ . \tag{34}$$

Since the r_p's are determinable from the equations already given, the terms on the left-hand side of the equation indicating the gold stocks of the respective countries can be evaluated and then summed to give the total monetary gold stock of the world.

After a serious disturbance, a return to an equilibrium which involves the equalization of the supply of and demand for gold as defined above might be reached only after a long process of adjustment. For the gold stock of the world is large relative to the changes in it which could readily be brought about through increased production and decreased consumption in the arts, or vice versa. Consequently, in the analysis of the effects of disturbances, especially for short periods of time, it may be advisable to neglect gold as an internationally traded commodity and deal only with relative prices. Another alternative is to modify the system of equations so as to represent the monetary gold stock of the world as roughly constant for purposes of studying its distribution among the various countries and its effects upon their price levels. The supply and demand for gold, *as we have defined them*, would then show an excess or deficit which would be absorbed by the world gold stock without, it may be assumed, appreciable effect on prices in the short run. The equations of Set I and that of Set II for gold would, of course, have to be adjusted to allow for this altered absorption of gold in the various gold-standard countries in excess or deficit of the amount indicated by the demand functions as they have been defined.

Our treatment of gold, money, and money prices has been restricted to the requirements of our immediate problem. We have not attempted to deal with the relation of the "productive service" of money to the rate of interest, one of the most perplexing points in the analyses of Pareto and his followers.[1]

[1] See Appendix II, the section on Pareto.

CHAPTER III

RELAXING THE LIMITATIONS ON THE EQUILIBRIUM EQUATIONS

1. INTRODUCTION

The limiting assumptions under which the results of the preceding chapter were obtained may be considerably relaxed, as was suggested, if appropriate changes be made in the equilibrium equations. Such modifications permit the recognition, in a more or less restricted way, of invisible items, duties, bounties, transportation costs, interdependence of the price-quantity relations of different commodities, i.e., rival or complementary demand and supply, non-uniformity in monetary shifts of the various schedules, and a monopoly in the supply of any commodity.

2. SERVICES IN THE INTERNATIONAL BALANCE

Invisible items may be classified into three groups: (*a*) services, such as transportation, insurance, services for foreign tourists, bankers' services, etc.; (*b*) credit transactions; (*c*) unilateral payments without a *quid pro quo*, such as indemnities, gifts, etc.

Services may be treated exactly as commodities, with a demand and a supply schedule in each country for each particular type of service. For many items in this class—e.g., transportation, insurance, and bankers' services—the demand is joint with the demand for commodities; in some instances, problems of joint supply arise. Rival and complementary relationships are not, however, peculiar to service items; they are also characteristic of commodities. Methods of dealing with them are suggested in the portions of this chapter which are concerned with transportation costs and the general interdependence of the price-quantity relations for different commodities.

3. CREDIT TRANSACTIONS AND UNILATERAL PAYMENTS

Groups (b) and (c) may be combined. The transfer of the proceeds of a loan or the repayment of earlier borrowings is analogous to the transfer of an indemnity as regards immediate effects upon the *status quo* in international trade. Both loans and unilateral payments tend to create an increase of circulating money media in the country receiving them and a decrease of circulating money media in the country making them. In the following analysis it will be assumed that these increases or decreases of circulating media are generalized so that all the demand and supply schedules of a country for internationally traded commodities tend to rise or fall by the same ratio.

If the net amount of loans and unilateral items may be treated as constant—and we shall limit the discussion to this case—it is usually constant in terms of convertible money rather than when deflated to the basis on which the fixed-height schedules are defined. If, however, these net amounts for the various countries were constant on the fixed-schedule basis for any country or countries, they could be dealt with very simply. Instead of the equations of Set I (III, IV, V), (22), which indicate the (deflated) total of export ($+$) and import ($-$) values, having zeros on the right-hand side, they would have constants (or constants with appropriate $\frac{z_1}{p}$ multipliers and/or divisors) with proper signs. The adjustment of the conditions of commodity trade to offset the net amounts of loans and other invisible items is given by the solution of these equations together with those of Set II (IV, V), (24).

In the more probable case with the net amount of loans and unilateral items constant in convertible money the procedure is slightly different. As an illustration, let us take the case of an indemnity payable by country 2 to country 1 in terms of country 1's currency, $I_{(1\leftarrow 2)}$. Deflated to the monetary conditions of fixed-height schedules, this would be for country 1,

$$\frac{I_{(1\leftarrow 2)}}{r_1},$$

or for country 2,

$$\frac{I_{(1\leftarrow2)}c_{\frac{1}{2}}}{r_2} = \frac{I_{(1\leftarrow2)}z_{\frac{1}{2}}}{r_1}.$$

The equations of Set I (III, IV, V), (22), would then be (m equations):

For country 1,

$$\sum_{i=1}^{i=n} y_{1i}f_{1i}(y_{1i}) = -\frac{I_{(1\leftarrow2)}}{r_1}.\tag{35}$$

For country 2,

$$\sum_{i=1}^{i=n} y_{1i}f_{2i}(z_{\frac{1}{2}}y_{1i}) = +\frac{I_{(1\leftarrow2)}z_{\frac{1}{2}}}{r_1z_{\frac{1}{2}}} = +\frac{I_{(1\leftarrow2)}}{r_1}.\tag{36}$$

For countries 3 to m,

$$\sum_{i=1}^{i=n} y_{1i}f_{pi}(z_1 y_{1i}) = 0.\tag{37}$$

The equations of Set II (IV, V), (24), must be included (n equations):

$$\sum_{i=1}^{i=m} f_{ik}(z_1 y_{1k}) = 0.\tag{38}$$

If commodity 1 is gold, we may substitute in equations (36), (37), and (38) $\dfrac{Y_{11}}{r_1}$ for y_{11}. The solution will then be determinate, since Y_{11} is a constant.

UNKNOWNS

Symbol	Number
r_1	1
y_{12} to y_{1n}	$n-1$
z_1	$m-1$
	$m+n-1$

EQUATIONS

Set	Number
Set I (III, IV, V), (35), (36), (37),............m	
Set II (IV, V), (38),.........................n	

$$m+n$$

But of the $(m+n)$ equations in Set I (III, IV, V) and Set II (IV, V), one is determinable when the other $(m+n-1)$ are given, so that there is the same number of independent equations as unknowns.

4. PROHIBITIONS, DUTIES, AND BOUNTIES

Artificial impediments to trade and the converse, special inducements, may be divided into two classes: outright prohibitions of exports or imports, and duties and bounties.

Prohibition of imports or exports of a specific commodity into or from a given country is easily recognized by simply setting the x_{pk}, and hence the $x_{pk}y_{pk}$, in question equal to zero. Prohibitions of imports from, or exports to, a few specific countries cannot be dealt with in our system of equations. In the absence of other impediments to trade and with multiple sources of supply and demand for the commodities in question, such discrimination would be thwarted by simple shifts in the buyer-seller relations. If other impediments do exist, this discrimination depends for its effectiveness on the absence of other large, elastic sources of supply (or large elastic demands) which are in actual competition with the supply (or demand) of the country attempting the discrimination.

Duties and bounties must be classified for treatment as ad valorem and specific. We shall assume that the proceeds of duties are expended, and the funds for bounties are secured, in such manner that the effects are generally distributed and all the schedules of the country tend to be raised, or lowered, by the same ratio.

If there is an ad valorem duty, T, on commodity k imported into the pth country and if the full duty-paid price on the fixed schedule is represented by y_{pk}, the price less the duty, still on the fixed schedule, is $\dfrac{y_{pk}}{1+T}$, $(=z_1 y_{1k})$. The total value which must be paid to foreign countries for the imports is, on the fixed schedule basis, $\dfrac{y_{pk}}{1+T}\,x_{pk}$ or $z_1 y_{1k} f_{pk}[z_1 y_{1k}(1+T)]$. To adapt the equations of Set I (III, IV, V), (22), and Set II (IV, V), (24), it is therefore only necessary to change $f_{pk}(z_1 y_{1k})$ to $f_{pk}[z_1 y_{1k}(1+T)]$ for the taxed commodity. An ad valorem bounty on exports, B, if one were offered, would be dealt with in exactly the same way, with the insertion of the factor $(1+B)$ in place of $(1+T)$.

A specific duty or bounty is a fixed *money* amount per unit of a commodity imported or exported. If the specific duty on the kth commodity imported into country p is T' in the currency of that country, it would on the fixed-schedule basis be equivalent to $\dfrac{T'}{r_p}$. If the fixed-schedule price including duty is indicated by y_{pk}, the corresponding price less duty is $\left(y_{pk}-\dfrac{T'}{r_p}\right)$, $(=z_1 y_{1k})$, and the total payment to other countries is $\left(y_{pk}-\dfrac{T'}{r_p}\right)x_{pk}$, or $z_1 y_{1k} f_{pk}\left[z_1 y_{1k}+\dfrac{T'}{r_p}\right]$. Remembering the changed relation between y_{pk} and y_{1k}, it is only necessary for us to rewrite the equilibrium equations of Sets I (III, IV, V), (22), and II (IV, V), (24), inserting $f_{pk}\left(z_1 y_{1k}+\dfrac{T'}{r_p}\right)$ in place of $f_{pk}(z_1 y_{1k})$ for the taxed commodity. This r_p might be a known constant; but if p is a gold-standard country, it is better regarded as a variable and we might therefore modify the system of equations, as indicated in section 9 of chapter ii, by the recognition of gold as a commodity of fixed money price in gold-standard countries. A specific bounty, B', would be dealt with as above with the B' replacing the T'.

5. TRANSPORTATION COSTS

If both natural and artificial impediments to trade were absent, every commodity would (except in rare instances) be either imported or exported to some extent—purely domestic commodities would be practically non-existent. The impediments to trade—of which cost of transportation is the greatest—create the gap between the prices at which imports of a commodity cease and exports begin. The effects of transportation costs upon economic phenomena have been too much neglected, and their inclusion in mathematical descriptions of equilibrium has not usually been attempted. We shall give particular attention to transportation services because their cost is so important an obstacle to trade and because the demand for and the supply of these services are excellent illustrations of joint demand and joint supply.

With the introduction of transportation costs, the description of equilibrium becomes much more complex. The uniformity of international prices must now be modified to allow for costs of carriage. And the number of possible routes of transportation between countries is enormous if the countries are numerous. But the chief difficulty is encountered in a perfectly general set of equilibrium equations because it cannot be ascertained in advance which commodities are imported into, and which are exported from, each country.

To avoid some of these complications, we shall make no attempt to introduce transportation costs into a thoroughly general system of equilibrium equations. Instead, we shall simplify the problem by assuming that we know whether each commodity is imported into or exported from each country and to which countries the exports of each country go—or, its equivalent, from which countries the imports of each country come. We shall also neglect the internal transportation costs and the geographical variations in conditions of supply and demand within each country and shall regard each country spatially as a point.

If all types of transportation services have horizontal supply curves and it is known on which commodities each country furnishes the carriage, the equilibrium equations for two countries are readily obtained. It is, in fact, possible to use the equilibrium equations as given in chapter ii with merely a *redefinition* of the y_{pk}'s. In such a case each y_{pk} would be the fixed-schedule import demand price, *less* the costs of transporting the commodity to the country *if* the importing country furnished the transport service, or the fixed schedule export supply price, *plus* the costs of carrying the commodity to the other country *if* the exporting country furnished the service.

From this ultra-simplified case we might proceed by successive stages to recognize: (*a*) variable transport costs, (*b*) the joint-cost characteristic of transportation as regards different commodities and different routes, and (*c*) additional countries. It will be quite as satisfactory and much briefer to give immediately an illustration involving three countries, three commodities, and costs of transportation which are both variable and joint. This illustration, it should be noted, exhibits all the types of relations existing in more extensive cases.

It is now necessary to distinguish the imports of a commodity which come from different countries. Thus if x_{11} be negative (imports of commodity 1 into country 1), we might have, for example,

$$x_{11} = x_{(1 \leftarrow 2)1} + x_{(1 \leftarrow 3)1} , \qquad (39)$$

in which $x_{(1 \leftarrow 2)1}$ would represent imports of commodity 1 (last subscript) into country 1 coming from country 2, and $x_{(1 \leftarrow 3)1}$ the imports from country 3. For exports of commodity 2 from country 1, $(x_{12} > 0)$, it might be true that

$$x_{12} = x_{(1 \rightarrow 2)2} + x_{(1 \rightarrow 3)2} , \qquad (40)$$

wherein $x_{(1\to 2)2}$ would be the exports of commodity 2 from country 1 to country 2, and $x_{(1\to 3)2}$ the exports to country 3. An arrow pointing to the left specifies an import $(-)$; and an arrow pointing to the right, an export $(+)$.

Let us suppose that the commodities are imported into or exported from the various countries as indicated by Figure 1. In it the countries are represented by the Roman numerals, the commodities by Arabic numerals, and the direction of shipment of the commodities by the arrows.

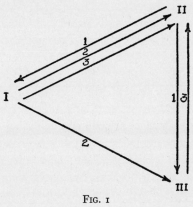

FIG. 1

This diagram is the equivalent of the following nine equations:

$$x_{11} = x_{(1\leftarrow 2)1} \cdot$$

$$x_{12} = x_{(1\to 2)2} + x_{(1\to 3)2} \cdot$$

$$x_{13} = x_{(1\to 2)3} \cdot$$

$$x_{21} = x_{(2\to 1)1} + x_{(2\to 3)1} \cdot$$

$$x_{22} = x_{(2\leftarrow 1)2} \cdot \qquad\qquad (41)$$

$$x_{23} = x_{(2\leftarrow 1)3} + x_{(2\leftarrow 3)3} \cdot$$

$$x_{31} = x_{(3\leftarrow 2)1} \cdot$$

$$x_{32} = x_{(3\leftarrow 1)2} \cdot$$

$$x_{33} = x_{(3\to 2)3} \cdot$$

But a quantity exported from one country is imported into another, so that the twelve quantities on the right-hand side of the foregoing equations are connected by the six equations:

$$x_{(1 \leftarrow 2)1} + x_{(2 \rightarrow 1)1} = 0 \; .$$

$$x_{(1 \rightarrow 2)2} + x_{(2 \leftarrow 1)2} = 0 \; .$$

$$x_{(1 \rightarrow 3)2} + x_{(3 \leftarrow 1)2} = 0 \; .$$

$$x_{(1 \rightarrow 2)3} + x_{(2 \leftarrow 1)3} = 0 \; .$$ \hfill (42)

$$x_{(2 \rightarrow 3)1} + x_{(3 \leftarrow 2)1} = 0 \; .$$

$$x_{(2 \leftarrow 3)3} + x_{(3 \rightarrow 2)3} = 0 \; .$$

Let us recognize as an individual "commodity" the transportation service for each tangible commodity over each separate route of shipment. In Figure 1 there are six such commodity routes. Let the unit of service in each instance be that necessary to carry one unit of the specified commodity over the specified route. Then the total quantity of transportation service required to carry the kth commodity from country p to country p' is equal in magnitude with the number of units of commodity transported, i.e., $x_{(p \rightarrow p')k}$. By analogy with earlier notation, the portion of this service furnished by country p'' would be $q_{s,p''t_{(p \rightarrow p')k}}$, and the price of this service on the fixed-height schedule of country p'' would be $y_{p''t_{(p \rightarrow p')k}}$.

For the six commodity routes as shown in Figure 1 there are six equations stating that the total quantity of each type of transportation service is equal to the sum of the quantities furnished by each of the three countries:

$$x_{(p \rightarrow p')k} = \sum_{i=1}^{i=3} q_{s,it_{(p \rightarrow p')k}} \; .$$ \hfill (43)

This equation recognizes that the demand for transportation services is joint with the demand for the commodity carried.

The quantity of each type of transportation service furnished by each country is a function of the prices of all the various types of transportation service—a statement which covers the joint supply characteristics of such services. This gives eighteen equations, six for each country. The general equations for the respective countries are:

$$q_{s,1t_{(p \to p')k}} = \psi_{s,1t_{(p \to p')k}} \left(\cdots y_{1t_{(j \to i')i}} \cdots \right) .$$
$$q_{s,2t_{(p \to p')k}} = \psi_{s,2t_{(p \to p')k}} \left(\cdots y_{2t_{(j \to i')i}} \cdots \right) . \qquad (44)$$
$$q_{s,3t_{(p \to p')k}} = \psi_{s,3t_{(p \to p')k}} \left(\cdots y_{3t_{(j \to i')i}} \cdots \right) .$$

The equality of international prices of transport services is assumed. This leads to twelve equations, six each of the two types,

$$z_{\frac{1}{2}} = \frac{y_{2t_{(p \to p')k}}}{y_{1t_{(p \to p')k}}} .$$

$$z_{\frac{1}{3}} = \frac{y_{3t_{(p \to p')k}}}{y_{1t_{(p \to p')k}}} . \qquad (45)$$

To describe the relations between prices in the various countries when transportation costs have been taken into consideration, the following six equations are required:

$$z_{\frac{1}{2}} = \frac{y_{21} + y_{2t_{(2 \to 1)1}}}{y_{11}} .$$

$$z_{\frac{1}{2}} = \frac{y_{22} - y_{2t_{(1 \to 2)2}}}{y_{12}} .$$

$$z_{\frac{1}{2}} = \frac{y_{23} - y_{2t_{(1 \to 2)3}}}{y_{13}} .$$

$$z_{\frac{1}{3}} = \frac{y_{31} + \left(y_{3t_{(2 \to 1)1}} - y_{3t_{(2 \to 3)1}} \right)}{y_{11}} . \qquad (46)$$

$$z_{\frac{1}{3}} = \frac{y_{32} - y_{3t_{(1 \to 3)2}}}{y_{12}} .$$

$$z_{\frac{1}{3}} = \frac{y_{33} + \left(y_{3t_{(3 \to 2)3}} - y_{3t_{(1 \to 2)3}} \right)}{y_{13}} .$$

The other equations necessary to complete the system are the nine equations of Set IV, (17),

$$x_{pk} = f_{pk}(y_{pk}) \ , \qquad\qquad (47)$$

and the three equations which express for each country the equality of the values of imports (c.i.f.) to the values of exports (f.o.b.) plus the value of transportation services furnished,

$$x_{11}y_{11} + x_{12}y_{12} + x_{13}y_{13} + \sum \left(q_{s,1t_{(j \to i')i}} y_{1t_{(j \to i')i}} \right) = 0 \ .$$
$$x_{21}y_{21} + x_{22}y_{22} + x_{23}y_{23} + \sum \left(q_{s,2t_{(j \to i')i}} y_{2t_{(j \to i')i}} \right) = 0 \ . \qquad (48)$$
$$x_{31}y_{31} + x_{32}y_{32} + x_{33}y_{33} + \sum \left(q_{s,3t_{(j \to i')i}} y_{3t_{(j \to i')i}} \right) = 0 \ .$$

In each of these equations the summation for the value of transportation services furnished extends over all the individual commodity-routes, i.e., the six indicated in Figure 1.

The unknowns in this system are:

Symbol of Unknown	Number of Unknowns
x_{pk}	9
$x_{(p \to p')k}$ and $x_{(p \leftarrow p')k}$	12
$y_{pk}, \ (k \not\equiv t)$	9
$y_{pt_{(p \to p')k}}$	18
$z_{\frac{1}{p}}$	2
$q_{s,1t_{(p \to p')k}}, \ q_{s,2t_{(p \to p')k}}, \ q_{s,3t_{(p \to p')k}}$	18
Total number of unknowns	68

The equations relating these unknowns to each other are as follows:

Type of Equation	Number of Equations
(41)	9
(42)	6
(43)	6
(44)	18
(45)	12
(46)	6
(47)	9
(48)	3
Total number of equations	69

But from sets (41), (42), and (48) one equation can be eliminated, leaving 68 independent equations. We have consequently a determinate solution with the same number of equations as unknowns.

6. GENERALIZATION OF DEMAND AND SUPPLY FUNCTIONS

Except in the preceding illustration, it has been assumed thus far that each quantity of a commodity imported or exported is a function only of the price of that commodity (on the fixed-height schedules). It is easy to extend this functional relation so as to allow for the recognition of competing and complementary relations between commodities (inclusive of services). If the kth commodity is interdependent only with certain other internationally traded commodities and not at all with domestic commodities, the expression, $x_{pk} = f_{pk}(y_{pk})$, need merely be generalized:

$$x_{pk} = f_{pk}(y_{p1},\ y_{p2},\ \ldots\ldots\ y_{pk}\ \ldots\ldots\ y_{pn})\ . \tag{49}$$

The prices of purely domestic commodities, for which we may use the general symbol, $y'_{pk'}$, may also be brought into the functional relation. Thus, if the quantity of commodity k is in part a function of the price of the k'th domestic commodity, we should have:

$$x_{pk} = f_{pk}(y_{p1},\ y_{p2},\ \ldots\ldots\ y_{pk}\ \ldots\ldots\ y_{pn},\ y'_{pk'})\ . \tag{50}$$

But since another variable has been introduced, another equation will be needed for a solution. This will be of the type,

$$\psi_{d,pk'}(y'_{pk'}) = \psi_{s,pk'}(y'_{pk'},\ y_{pk})\ , \tag{51}$$

if the supply of the domestic commodity is related to y_{pk}, or

$$\psi_{d,pk'}(y'_{pk'},\ y_{pk}) = \psi_{s,pk'}(y'_{pk'})\ , \tag{52}$$

if the demand for the domestic commodity is related to y_{pk}. Equations (51) and (52) might be more complicated, involving additional prices; but the procedure in general is simple. For every domestic price brought into the system an equation of the general type (51) or (52) is necessary, equating the quantity of the domestic commodity demanded to the quantity supplied.

7. EXCLUSION OF FACTORS OF PRODUCTION

As was pointed out in the first chapter, still further generality may be achieved by bringing into the system the factors of production and the whole set of purely domestic prices and quantities for each country. In such a step one would not encounter any peculiar theoretical difficulties demanding special consideration here, but the complexities of notation and the increases in the number of unknowns and equations would be very great. By excluding the equations involving the factors of production and assuming definite supply functions instead, we are, of course, prevented from investigating the behavior of the factors of production in international trade. We do not thereby mean to imply that they are not worth studying. But it seemed doubtful whether it would be profitable to adopt the mathematical method in such a study, except, perhaps, merely to state the general conditions of equilibrium. By restricting the scope of our equations, we are able to make use of them in the solution of some important problems.

8. DYNAMIC MONETARY CHANGES

If the mechanisms of adjustment of international balances of debits and credits involve only the exchange rates and not the price level, our assumption of frictionless operation of these mechanisms is a fair approximation to reality. For the exchange rate is sensitive and, when it is modified, does have very nearly the effect of a uniform change in the net monetary factor $\frac{z_1}{p}$ for all commodities. On the other hand, when adjustment to equilibrium is achieved by, or even accompanied by, general shifts in the height of the demand and supply schedules, such shifts are apt to be somewhat irregular during transition. They do, however,

tend to approximate uniformity if new disturbing elements do
not enter.

For study of the effects of disturbances to equilibrium when the
shifts in the schedule are not proportionally equal, the reader is
referred to section 4 of chapter v.

9. MONOPOLY

The alterations in the equilibrium equations necessary to
describe the operations of a monopoly, which is free to charge
different prices in different markets, are worth considering. In
the five sets of equilibrium equations in chapter ii, (14), (15),
(16), (17), (18), which may be written for three countries trading
in n commodities, competitive conditions were assumed. Now let
us assume, instead, that the first commodity is controlled by a
monopoly in country 2 and exported to countries 1 and 3, which
may or may not have competing domestic producers, and then
observe the changes which are required. In the first place, the
two fundamental equations in international trade exhibiting the
equality of values of imports and exports for each country and the
equality of quantities of imports and exports for each commodity
are unaffected (Sets I and II). So also are the equations of Set III
in which the actual price Y_{pk} is equated to a ratio r_p times the
fixed-height schedule price y_{pk}. The equations of Set IV express
the quantity of imports which would be taken or exports which
would be offered as a function of the fixed schedule price. A simple functional relation between the quantity offered by a monopoly and its price does not exist; and consequently we must drop
out the equation,

$$x_{21} = f_{21}(y_{21}) . \tag{53}$$

The equations of Set V are based on the equality of the prices of
a commodity in all countries and would not hold for commodity 2.
Thus we lose the two equations,

$$y_{21} = z_{\frac{1}{2}} y_{11} .$$
$$y_{31} = z_{\frac{1}{3}} y_{11} . \tag{54}$$

In all we lose three equations of this system for competition. These are replaced by the six following equations of which the first two, (3) and (1), have already been given. The third of these expresses the average unit cost of production by the monopoly as a function of its output.

$$q_{s,21} - q_{d,21} = x_{21} \ . \tag{55}$$

$$q_{d,21} = \psi_{d,21}(y_{21}) \ . \tag{56}$$

$$y_{c,21} = f_{21}(q_{s,21}) \ . \tag{57}$$

The remaining three equations are peculiar to a monopoly which can discriminate in price between markets.[1] They state the condition that the marginal or differential gross revenue *to the monopoly* from the sale of an additional unit in each market must be the same and must be equal to the marginal cost of production.

$$\frac{d(q_{d,21}y_{21})}{dq_{d,21}} = \frac{d(x_{11}z_{\frac{1}{2}}y_{11})}{dx_{11}} = \frac{d\left(x_{31}\dfrac{z_{\frac{1}{2}}}{z_{\frac{1}{3}}}y_{31}\right)}{dx_{31}} = \frac{d(q_{s,21}y_{c,21})}{dq_{s,21}} \ . \tag{58}$$

In the differentiation the z's may be regarded as constant if the monopoly neglects the effects of its own action on the relative price levels and exchange rates.

We have in these six additional equations introduced the three additional unknowns $q_{s,21}$, $q_{d,21}$, and $y_{c,21}$, so that we have left a net of three equations to compensate for the three equations which were dropped from the competitive system. The solution, therefore, remains determinate.

[1] T. O. Yntema, "The Influence of Dumping on Monopoly Price," *Journal of Political Economy*, XXXVI (1928), 687–89.

CHAPTER IV

GRAPHIC METHODS

1. DEFINITION OF IMPORT DEMAND AND EXPORT SUPPLY

The algebraic analysis of the preceding chapter suggests comments on some of the graphic methods in current use[1] and also the possibility of a new graphic treatment.

In equations (1), (2), (3), (4), and (5) of chapter ii the functional relation of the quantity of a commodity exported or imported to its price, when the schedules are at some fixed height, was defined as

$$x_{pk} = q_{s,pk} - q_{d,pk} = \psi_{s,pk}(y_{pk}) - \psi_{d,pk}(y_{pk}) = f_{pk}(y_{pk}) , \qquad (59)$$

except for *imports* of a commodity which, if it were produced domestically, would be supplied at decreasing price. Under this exceptional condition,

$$x_{pk} = 0 - q_{d,pk} = 0 - \psi_{d,pk}(y_{pk}) = f_{pk}(y_{pk}) , \qquad (60)$$

a relation which can be explained more satisfactorily after the graphic counterpart of the normal relations in (59) has been described.

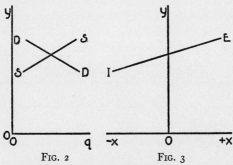

FIG. 2   FIG. 3

[1] Diagrams similar to many of those in this chapter are given in *Geometrical Political Economy* by H. Cunynghame. See Appendix I for comments on the graphic methods of Cunynghame, Auspitz and Lieben, and others.

In Figure 2 for the normal case let the supply function, $q_{s,pk} = \psi_{s,pk}(y_{pk})$, be represented by the line SS and the demand function, $q_{d,pk} = \psi_{d,pk}(y_{pk})$, be represented by the line DD. For successive values of y let the abscissa of DD be subtracted from the abscissa of SS, $(q_{s,pk} - q_{d,pk} = x_{pk})$, and let this difference be plotted against y_{pk} in Figure 3. Figure 3 therefore exhibits the graph of the function,

$$x_{pk} = f_{pk}(y_{pk}) , \tag{61}$$

in which positive values of x are quantities exported and negative values of x are quantities imported. The portion of the curve in Figure 3 which lies to the right of the origin is the export supply curve; and the portion to the left of the origin, the import demand curve. It should be observed that in this sort of a graph the import demand curve has negative values of x as abscissae and that its slope is positive.

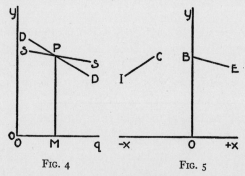

FIG. 4   FIG. 5

Figures 4 and 5, analogous to Figures 2 and 3, indicate the graphic treatment of the exceptional case. The right half of Figure 5, which relates to exports, does not come under the exceptional case and is obtained just as in Figure 3. To explain the left half of Figure 5, for imports, a statement of the significance of a negatively sloped supply curve is required. The abscissa of any point on a negatively sloped supply curve indicates the *smallest* quantity which will be supplied at the stated price (whereas the abscissa of any point on a positively sloped supply curve is the largest quantity which will be supplied at the stated price). If any imports reach the domestic market, they will enter at a price below *PM*. But if the price falls below *PM*, the sales of producers in the domestic market will necessarily be less than the minimum quantity which they will supply at such a price. Consequently, domestic producers will be forced out of business and the whole supply will be imported. The discontinuity from *B* to *C* in Figure 5 results from the fact that domestic and foreign producers cannot share the domestic market under such conditions.[1]

2. ELASTICITY OF IMPORT DEMAND AND EXPORT SUPPLY

It is possible—and useful—to deal with elasticities of import demand and of export supply, defined in both cases as

$$h_{pk} = \left(\frac{y}{x} \frac{dx}{dy} \right)_{pk}. \tag{62}$$

The subscripts outside parentheses or brackets signify that all the variables and functions therein should bear these subscripts. If it is desired to indicate that h_{pk} refers to export supply (or to import demand), it may be written $h_{s,pk}$ (or $h_{d,pk}$).

But this elasticity, h_{pk}, must be sharply distinguished from the elasticity of domestic demand, η_{pk},

$$\eta_{pk} = \left(\frac{y}{q_d,} \frac{dq_d,}{dy} \right)_{pk} \tag{63}$$

and from the elasticity of domestic supply, e_{pk},

$$e_{pk} = \left(\frac{y}{q_s,} \frac{dq_s,}{dy} \right)_{pk}. \tag{64}$$

[1] I am indebted to Professor Viner for this treatment of the exceptional case.

The relations between these elasticities (save in the exceptional case, in which $h_{d,pk}$ is identical with η_{pk}) will be apparent from the following:

$$h_{pk} = \left(\frac{y}{x}\frac{dx}{dy}\right)_{pk} = \left(\frac{y}{q_{s,}-q_{d,}}\frac{d(q_{s,}-d_{d,})}{dy}\right)_{pk} =$$

$$\left[\frac{1}{q_{s,}-q_{d,}}\left(q_{s,}\frac{y}{q_{s,}}\frac{dq_{s,}}{dy}-q_{d,}\frac{y}{q_{d,}}\frac{dq_{d,}}{dy}\right)\right]_{pk} =$$

$$\left(\frac{eq_{s,}-\eta q_{d,}}{q_{s,}-q_{d,}}\right)_{pk}. \qquad (65)$$

Formula (65) and all other formulas for elasticities involving η_{pk} and e_{pk} may be adapted to the exceptional case, for *imports*, by simply setting the $q_{s,}$ in the formula equal to zero.

From (65) it is clear that if $e_{pk} > 0$, then $|h_{pk}|$, the absolute magnitude of the elasticity of import demand or export supply, is greater, the larger are the absolute values of e_{pk}, η_{pk}, $q_{s,pk}$, and $q_{d,pk}$, and the smaller is the absolute difference $|q_{s,pk}-q_{d,pk}|$, which is the quantity imported or exported. Thus, if for sugar in the United States, $\eta = -0.5$, $e = +0.5$, and the domestic consumption, $q_{d,}$, is twice the domestic supply, $q_{s,}$,

$$h = \frac{0.5q_{s,}-[-0.5(2q_{s,})]}{q_{s,}-2q_{s,}} = \frac{0.5+1}{-1} = -1.5. \qquad (66)$$

Whereas the elasticity of domestic demand is -0.5, the elasticity of demand for *imports* is -1.5, a striking contrast. So long as we are dealing with conditions of increasing cost in a country, $(e>0)$, inelastic demands for imports will be relatively rare if there is a domestic industry of any size competing with the imports. Analogously, if $e>0$, the elasticity of export supply will exceed the elasticity, e, of the whole domestic supply by a difference which is greater the larger is the domestic consumption. The tendency toward high elasticities of export supply is lessened by different producers specializing in foreign and domestic markets respectively, especially if there are serious obstacles to shifting sales from one market to another. For export staples of the United States, in which the domestic market is large and the obstacles to shifting from one market to another not important, the elasticity of export supply must be high. The significance of high elasticities in international trade should not be overlooked, for they tend to lessen the price changes and the shifts of schedules which are necessary in adjustments to equilibrium.

3. EFFECTS OF IMPEDIMENTS ON IMPORT DEMAND AND EXPORT SUPPLY CURVES

The way in which duties modify the effective import demand or export supply is exhibited in Figures 6 and 7. In Figure 6 an

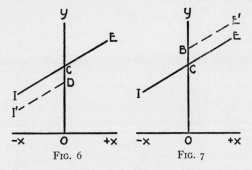

FIG. 6   FIG. 7

import duty drops the left half of the curve (import demand) from IC to $I'D$. In Figure 7 an export duty raises the right half of the curve of export supply from CE to BE'. An export bounty would have had the opposite effect, that of lowering CE, the curve of export supply. As a result of a specific bounty or duty, the curve would be shifted by a constant vertical distance—if the general changes in the height of the country's demand and supply schedules might be neglected. Strictly, of course, the money duty should be deflated by a variable—but this variable deflating factor, r_p, cannot be ascertained in advance. Consequently, in using the graphic method it is not possible to represent exactly the effect of a specific duty or bounty. The effect of an ad valorem duty (or bounty) would be to shift the schedule by a constant percentage of its ordinate. It therefore can be represented without difficulty.

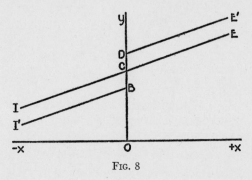

Fig. 8

Figure 8 illustrates the effects of transportation costs which are constant when deflated to the basis of definition of the fixed-height schedules and uniform for all imports of the commodity. The curve of import demand at delivered prices is IC, but at prices f.o.b. the exporting country is $I'B$. The curve of export supply at f.o.b. prices is CE but at delivered prices is DE'.

In Figures 6 and 7 (which neglect transportation costs) there exists a gap, resulting from a duty, between the highest effective import demand price and the lowest effective export supply price. In Figure 8 there is a similar gap, due to costs of transportation, between the highest import demand price and the lowest export supply price which are effective *at the foreign country's point of shipment and receipt*. When duties (bounties may be regarded as negative duties) and costs of transportation are combined, their effect is, of course, additive. Now it is apparent that if the foreign price falls within such a gap, the commodity will not be exported or imported but will be purely a domestic product. Further, it appears that there can be a difference between the prices of domestic commodities in the respective countries ranging from zero to the difference between the lowest export supply price and the highest import demand price of one country effective at the point of shipment and receipt of the other country.

4. DERIVATION OF MARSHALL'S CURVES OF INTERNATIONAL TRADE

The most successful graphic analysis of the problems in international trade theory has been that devised by Alfred Marshall.[1]

The relation of Marshall's curves to the ordinary domestic demand and supply curves does not seem to be generally known, and it appears desirable to explain their derivation and their relation to our algebraic statement. For graphic treatment Marshall reduces all imports to a representative unit (bale of imports) and all exports likewise to a representative unit (bale of exports). If the difficulties implicit in this procedure be waived or, better, if there be only two simple commodities traded between the two countries, the equations expressing the equality of values of exports and imports (for fixed-height schedules) may be written:

$$x_{11}y_{11} + x_{12}y_{12} = 0 \tag{67}$$

$$x_{21}y_{21} + x_{22}y_{22} = 0 \tag{68}$$

or

$$x_{11}\phi_{11}(x_{11}) + x_{12}\phi_{12}(x_{12}) = 0 . \tag{69}$$

$$x_{21}\phi_{21}(x_{21}) + x_{22}\phi_{22}(x_{22}) = 0 . \tag{70}$$

From (69) are deducible the series of pairs of x_{11} and x_{12} quantities, for which (neglecting signs) the values of the imports of one commodity would equal the values of exports of the other commodity. When x_{11} is negative, representing imports, and x_{12} is positive, representing exports, they are (now neglecting their signs) the co-ordinates of a Marshallian curve of demand of country 1 for commodity 1 in terms of commodity 2. When x_{11} is positive, repre-

[1] Alfred Marshall, *The Pure Theory of Foreign Trade*, privately printed in 1879 and reprinted for publication in 1930. Marshall reproduced the substance of this essay in *Money, Credit and Commerce*, Appendix J.

senting exports, and x_{12} is negative, representing imports, they are the co-ordinates of a curve of demand for commodity 2 in terms of commodity 1. Similarly from (70) the demand curves of country 2 for commodity 2 in terms of commodity 1, and for commodity 1 in terms of 2, can be ascertained. Now, of all the double pairs of (x_{11}, x_{12}) and (x_{21}, x_{22}) values, that set provides the solution which satisfies the equations

$$x_{11} + x_{21} = 0 .\tag{71}$$

$$x_{12} + x_{22} = 0 .\tag{72}$$

If we construct a graph, one of whose axes represents $(-x_{11})$, imports into country 1 of commodity 1, and $(+x_{21})$, exports from country 2 of commodity 1, and the other of whose axes represents $(+x_{12})$, exports from country 1 of commodity 2, and $(-x_{22})$, imports into country 2 of commodity 2, we can plot the two Marshallian demand curves and have their intersection determine the quantities imported and exported. Each of these Marshallian curves would then appear in both the first and third quadrants. But the axes are usually arbitrarily defined so as to bring the point of intersection into the first quadrant, and the portions of the curves outside this quadrant are omitted.

The graphic derivation of Marshall's curves is as follows.[1] In Figure 9 are given the domestic demand and supply curves of country 1 for commodities 1 and 2. The series of $(-x_{11})$ and x_{12} quantities necessary to construct a Marshallian curve for coun-

---

[1] This derivation is based on the assumption that the import demand price on its fixed-height schedule is a function only of quantity imported and that the export supply price on its fixed-height schedule is a function only of quantity exported. Marshall's comments on the interdependence of import demand and export supply seem to refer not to a functional interrelation of fixed-height schedules but to the interdependence which arises out of the necessity of balancing international debits and credits. Where a functional relation between fixed-height schedules does exist, Marshall's curves are still applicable, but they cannot be derived from their component elements by two-dimensional graphics.

try 1 representing the import demand for commodity 1 in terms of commodity 2 are such values of a_1b_1 and a_2b_2 as would yield equal areas for $d_1c_1b_1a_1$ and $d_2c_2b_2a_2$, or, in other words, would equate the values of imports and exports. If a_1b_1 rises above the point of intersection of $D_{11}D_{11}$ and $S_{11}S_{11}$, and if a_2b_2 falls below the point of intersection, the resulting portion of the Marshallian curve represents the demand of country 1 for commodity 2 in

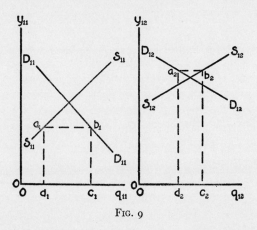

FIG. 9

terms of commodity 1. Similar curves are obtainable for the second country. When the curves for both countries are plotted, they will appear like those in Figure 10. Figure 11, bearing Marshall's notation, is identical with the first quadrant of Figure 10. In Figure 10 distances along the horizontal axis represent quantities of imports or exports of commodity 2 and along the vertical axis quantities of imports or exports of commodity 1. The curve $OD_{1\frac{1}{2}}$ represents the import demand of country 1 (first subscript) for commodity 1 (upper second subscript) in terms of commodity 2 (lower second subscript). From the other point of view, it represents the supply of commodity 2 in terms of 1. $OD_{2\frac{2}{1}}$ is for country 2 the curve of import demand for commodity 2 in terms of 1, or of export supply of commodity 1 in terms of 2. For the sake of completeness the curves $OD_{1\frac{2}{1}}$ and $OD_{2\frac{1}{2}}$ are shown in the third quadrant, although the portion of the curves of practical interest is that in the vicinity of the point of intersection, A.

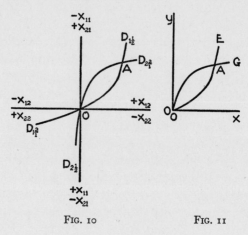

FIG. 10   FIG. 11

5. EFFECTS OF LOANS, DUTIES, BOUNTIES, ETC., ON THE MARSHALLIAN CURVES

These curves may still be constructed even though loans and unilateral items enter into the trade balances, provided that the balance of value of such items is constant under the monetary conditions maintaining the schedules at fixed heights. Although this could not be true for both countries if the net monetary factor, $z_{\frac{1}{2}}$, changed, such an assumption would be roughly correct if this change were not great. The net balance with the appropriate sign, deflated to the basis on which the schedules were defined for the respective countries, need merely be inserted as constants in equations (67) and (68). Graphically, the difference between the areas $d_1c_1b_1a_1$ and $d_2c_2b_2a_2$, Figure 9, must be kept equal to this constant value balance of invisible items. The rest of the procedure is unmodified.

The effect of duties and bounties upon the Marshallian curves can also be seen from these elementary demand and supply curves

(Figure 9). A general import duty (assuming its expenditure to be distributed so that all demand and supply schedules tend to be raised or lowered by the same ratio) results in decreasing the area $d_1c_1b_1a_1$ through decreasing the height d_1a_1 by the amount of the duty. Since for a given quantity of imports, a_1b_1, the payment to the foreign country is less, the area $d_2c_2b_2a_2$ will be correspondingly decreased. By analogous procedure we could deal with an export duty or export bounty. The effects of duties and bounties (assuming increases or decreases in circulating media resulting proximately therefrom to be generally distributed) may be summarized as follows (in terms of prices and values on fixed-height schedules):

a) An import duty decreases the value which would be paid to foreigners for a *given* quantity of imports and hence the value of the exports which would be sent in payment for that quantity.

b) An export duty increases the value asked of foreigners for a *given* quantity of exports and hence the value of imports which would be received in payment for that quantity.

c) An export bounty decreases the value asked of foreigners for a *given* quantity of exports and hence the value of the imports which would be received in payment for that quantity.

It will be useful to remember that the value of exports is (save in the very exceptional, if not impossible, instance, which we shall disregard, when $o > e > -1$) an increasing function of quantity, and that the value of imports is an increasing function of quantity for elastic import demand but a decreasing function of quantity for inelastic import demand. We come therefore to these conclusions:

a) An import duty will decrease the quantity of exports offered in exchange for a given quantity of imports.

b) An export duty will, if the import demand is elastic, increase the quantity of imports obtainable for a given quantity of exports, but, if the import demand is inelastic, decrease this quantity of imports.

c) An export bounty will, if the import demand is elastic, decrease the quantity of imports obtainable for a given quantity of exports, but, if the import demand is inelastic, will increase this quantity of imports.

Consequently, a general import or export duty will, whatever be the elasticity of import demand, decrease the quantity of exports offered for a given quantity of imports, or will shift the curve *OE* in Figure 11 to the left or the curve *OG* downward.[1] An export bounty will increase the quantity of exports offered for a given quantity of imports and will move *OE* to the right or *OG* upward.

With certain modifications, the generalizations just cited would cover impediments arising from costs of service necessary to trade, such as transportation costs. If the country for which the curve is constructed furnished exactly the service required, the procedure would be unchanged. But if this country furnished less or more than the necessary service, allowance should be made for this excess or deficit in the equality of the balance of payments. Of course, any such service cost must not be counted twice; modification of only one of the curves of Figures 10 or 11 is necessary.

6. MARSHALL'S ELASTICITIES OF DEMAND AND SUPPLY IN INTERNATIONAL TRADE

Having shown how the Marshallian international trade curves are related to the domestic demand and supply functions, we may pass to a consideration of Marshall's concept of elasticity of demand in foreign trade.[2] This is obtained by substituting in the ordinary mathematical definition of elasticity of demand the quantity imported for the quantity taken and the ratio of quantity exported to quantity imported for the price. The elasticity of demand of country 1 for commodity 1 (imported) in terms of

---

[1] See Appendix II, section on Edgeworth, for his error in believing this to be a case of asymmetry rather than symmetry.

[2] Alfred Marshall, *Money, Credit and Commerce*, pp. 167 ff. and Appendix J, pp. 337–38 n.

commodity 2 (exported) is therefore (without the negative sign prefixed by Marshall to obtain a positive value for the elasticity):

$$E_{d,1\frac{1}{2}} = \frac{\left(\dfrac{x_{12}}{-x_{11}}\right)}{(-x_{11})}\frac{d(-x_{11})}{d\left(\dfrac{x_{12}}{-x_{11}}\right)} = \frac{x_{12}}{x_{11}\dfrac{dx_{12}}{dx_{11}} - x_{12}} = \frac{1}{\dfrac{x_{11}}{x_{12}}\dfrac{dx_{12}}{dx_{11}} - 1} . \quad (73)$$

The symbol $E_{d,1\frac{1}{2}}$ is used in place of Marshall's "e" because the latter would be confused with the elasticity of domestic supply. Since x_{12} has a varying exchange value in terms of commodities whose prices remain constant on fixed-height schedules (domestic commodities), the definition of the elasticity, $E_{d,}$, is quite different from the $h_{d,}$ for import demand or the η for domestic demand. Both of these postulate a constant exchange value of the means of payment in terms of commodities whose quantities taken and supplied, and therefore whose fixed-height schedule prices, remain constant.

It is important to know just how these various concepts are related. In (62), (63), (64), we gave definitions of η, e, and h, the last also in terms of η, e, $q_{s,}$, and $q_{d,}$. It remains merely to define Marshall's elasticity of foreign demand, $E_{d,}$, in terms of the foregoing symbols. From (67), or even from a similar equation with a constant term for invisible items, it follows that

$$d(x_{12}y_{12}) = -d(x_{11}y_{11}) . \quad (74)$$

$$\frac{dx_{12}}{dx_{11}} = -\frac{y_{11}\left(\dfrac{x_{11}}{y_{11}}\dfrac{dy_{11}}{dx_{11}} + 1\right)}{y_{12}\left(\dfrac{x_{12}}{y_{12}}\dfrac{dy_{12}}{dx_{12}} + 1\right)} = -\frac{y_{11}\left(\dfrac{1}{h_{11}} + 1\right)}{y_{12}\left(\dfrac{1}{h_{12}} + 1\right)} . \quad (75)$$

In the case we are to deal with, h_{11} refers to elasticity of import demand and may be written $h_{d,11}$, while h_{12} refers to export supply and may be written $h_{s,12}$.

Substituting in (73) from (75), we get for the elasticity of demand of country 1 for commodity 1 (imported) in terms of commodity 2 (exported):

$$E_{d,1\frac{1}{2}} = \cfrac{1}{-\cfrac{x_{11}y_{11}\left(\dfrac{1}{h_{d,11}}+1\right)}{x_{12}y_{12}\left(\dfrac{1}{h_{s,12}}+1\right)}-1} \, . \qquad (76)$$

If there are no invisible items, this becomes simply:

$$E_{d,1\frac{1}{2}} = \cfrac{1}{\cfrac{\dfrac{1}{h_{d,11}}+1}{\dfrac{1}{h_{s,12}}+1}-1} = \frac{h_{d,11}+h_{d,11}h_{s,12}}{h_{s,12}-h_{d,11}} \, . \qquad (77)$$

We can, if we wish, substitute in (76) the domestic elasticities in place of the h's from (65):

$$E_{d,1\frac{1}{2}} = \cfrac{1}{-\cfrac{x_{11}y_{11}[q_{s,}\,(e+1)-q_{d,}\,(\eta+1)]_{11}(eq_{s,}-\eta q_{d,})_{12}}{x_{12}y_{12}[q_{s,}\,(e+1)-q_{d,}\,(\eta+1)]_{12}(eq_{s,}-\eta q_{d,})_{11}}-1} \, , \qquad (78)$$

or, in the absence of invisible items,

$$E_{d,1\frac{1}{2}} = \cfrac{1}{\cfrac{[q_{s,}\,(e+1)-q_{d,}\,(\eta+1)]_{11}(eq_{s,}-\eta q_{d,})_{12}}{[q_{s,}\,(e+1)-q_{d,}\,(\eta+1)]_{12}(eq_{s,}-\eta q_{d,})_{11}}-1} \, . \qquad (79)$$

The subscripts to the brackets again indicate that all variables and functions contained therein should bear those subscripts.

In general the elasticity of import demand, $h_{d,}$, or, referred to country 1's demand for commodity 1, $h_{d,11}$, is not equivalent to Marshall's foreign trade elasticity of demand, $E_{d,}$, (here $E_{d,1\frac{1}{2}}$). If, however, the exported commodity be produced under conditions of constant cost and the elasticity of export supply be infinite ($h_{s,12}=\infty$), it can be seen from (77) that $h_{d,}$ is equal to $E_{d,}$.

This is to be expected, since under such conditions the exchange value of the second commodity, which is the means of payment, is constant in terms of other commodities of fixed price. If we restrict the discussion to cases of increasing domestic costs of production for both commodities, h_{s_i} is positive and h_{d_i} is negative. Then if $h_{d_i} < -1$ (elastic), inspection of (77) shows $E_{d_i} > h_{d_i}$ or $|E_{d_i}| < |h_{d_i}|$, i.e., Marshall's elasticity is less than our elasticity of import demand. If $h_{d_i} = -1$ (unitary elasticity), they are equal. If $0 > h_{d_i} > -1$ (inelastic), Marshall's elasticity is the greater. These conclusions again accord with general reasoning based on the varying exchange value of the second commodity and the increased, constant, or decreased quantities of this commodity which must be given to obtain an increased quantity of the imported commodity.

Marshall's definition of the elasticity of a country's "willingness to extend her sales"[1] is the counterpart of elasticity of supply, if quantity of exports be substituted for quantity offered and the ratio of the quantity imported to quantity exported be taken as the price. Calling this E_{s_i} (instead of Marshall's e'), we may represent the elasticity of export supply (Marshall does not use this word) for country 1 of commodity 2 in terms of commodity 1.

$$E_{s,1\frac{2}{1}} = \frac{(-x_{11})}{x_{12}\dfrac{d(-x_{11})}{dx_{12}} - (-x_{11})} = \frac{1}{\dfrac{x_{12}}{x_{11}}\dfrac{dx_{11}}{dx_{12}} - 1} = \frac{1}{-\dfrac{x_{12}y_{12}\left(\dfrac{1}{h_{s,12}} + 1\right)}{x_{11}y_{11}\left(\dfrac{1}{h_{d,11}} + 1\right)} - 1} \,. \quad (80)$$

If no invisible items exist,

$$E_{s,1\frac{2}{1}} = \frac{1}{\dfrac{\dfrac{1}{h_{s,12}} + 1}{\dfrac{1}{h_{d,11}} + 1} - 1} = \frac{h_{s,12} + h_{s,12}\,h_{d,11}}{h_{d,11} - h_{s,12}} \,. \quad (81)$$

[1] Alfred Marshall, *Money, Credit and Commerce*, p. 338 n.

If desired, substitution could easily be made for $h_{s,12}$ and $h_{d,11}$ in terms of domestic elasticities of demand and supply.

Marshall's case of "exceptional demand" clearly corresponds to our inelastic import demand coupled with domestic production (if there is any) characterized by a positively sloping supply curve. Marshall's case of "exceptional supply" involves domestic decreasing costs, i.e., a negatively sloping supply curve. The question of the stability of an equilibrium involving exceptional elasticities is considered by Marshall in Appendix J to his *Money, Credit and Commerce*. We shall treat the question by a different method in the next chapter.

In following Marshall's discussion of his special cases, some help may be secured from the definition of the slope of his curve representing the demand of country 1 for commodity 1 in terms of commodity 2. From (75) the expression for this slope is:

$$\frac{dx_{11}}{dx_{12}} = \frac{y_{12}\left(\dfrac{1}{h_{s,12}}+1\right)}{y_{11}\left(\dfrac{1}{h_{d,11}}+1\right)} . \tag{82}$$

If $h_{s,12} > 0$ or < -1, the numerator is positive. The denominator is positive if $h_{d,11} < -1$, but negative if $0 > h_{d,11} > -1$.

7. A NEW GRAPHIC SOLUTION

Another graphic solution for equilibrium in international trade, quite different from Marshall's, is possible. The equilibrium equations for two countries and n traded commodities are by (32), (31), and (15) of chapter ii, respectively:

Set I (III, VI), (2 equations)

$$x_{11}\phi_{11}(x_{11})+x_{12}\phi_{12}(x_{12})+ \ldots +x_{1n}\phi_{1n}(x_{1n})=0 .$$

$$\tag{83}$$

$$x_{21}\phi_{21}(x_{21})+x_{22}\phi_{22}(x_{22})+ \cdots +x_{2n}\phi_{2n}(x_{2n})=0 .$$

Set V (VI), (n equations)

$$z_{\frac{1}{2}} = \frac{\phi_{2k}(x_{2k})}{\phi_{1k}(x_{1k})} \cdot \tag{84}$$

Set II (n equations)

$$x_{11} + x_{21} = 0 \cdot$$
$$x_{12} + x_{22} = 0 \cdot \tag{85}$$
$$\cdot \quad \cdot \quad \cdot \quad \cdot \quad \cdot$$
$$x_{1n} + x_{2n} = 0 \cdot$$

By substitution from Set II all the x_{2k}'s may be eliminated from Set I (III, VI) and Set V (VI), giving

Set I (II, III, VI)

$$x_{11}\phi_{11}(x_{11}) + x_{12}\phi_{12}(x_{12}) + \cdots + x_{1n}\phi_{1n}(x_{1n}) = 0 \cdot \tag{86}$$

$$(-x_{11})\phi_{21}(-x_{11}) + (-x_{12})\phi_{22}(-x_{12}) + \cdots$$
$$+ (-x_{1n})\phi_{2n}(-x_{1n}) = 0 \cdot \tag{87}$$

Set V (II, VI)

$$z_{\frac{1}{2}} = \frac{\phi_{2k}(-x_{1k})}{\phi_{1k}(x_{1k})} \cdot \tag{88}$$

From this last Set V (II, VI) an x_{1k} quantity can be determined for every value of the net monetary factor $z_{\frac{1}{2}}$. For any $z_{\frac{1}{2}}$ the terms in (86) can therefore be evaluated, since the $x_{11}, x_{12}, \ldots x_{1n}$ are known. Obviously, that value of the net monetary factor $z_{\frac{1}{2}}$ will exist at equilibrium for which equation (86) holds, i.e., for which the sum of the values of imports ($-$) and exports ($+$) is zero. If the sum of the terms in (86) is plotted on the vertical scale against $z_{\frac{1}{2}}$ on the horizontal scale, equilibrium is determined for that $z_{\frac{1}{2}}$ value at which the line crosses the horizontal axis. As variants of this method it is possible to plot the sum of the exports and the sum of the imports separately, treating both as positive magnitudes, and letting their point of intersection locate the equilibrium value of $z_{\frac{1}{2}}$.

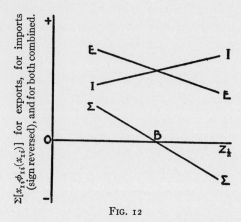

FIG. 12

In Figure 12 let EE represent the sum of the export values and II the sum of the import values as ascertained above. By subtracting the ordinate of II from that of EE, the ordinate of $\Sigma\Sigma$, i.e., $\left[\displaystyle\sum_{i=1}^{i=n} x_{1i}\phi_{1i}(x_{1i})\right]$, is secured. OB represents the equilibrium magnitude of the net monetary factor $z_{\frac{1}{2}}$. All the quantities of imports and exports, the x_{1k}'s and x_{2k}'s, are then determinable from the functions given, (88) and (85). The y_{1k}'s and y_{2k}'s are obtainable from the functional relation of price to quantity in each case, (6).

If all the import demands of both countries are elastic and there are no negatively sloping export supply curves, the graph has lines with slopes of the same signs[1] as those in Figure 12.

This method of presentation is less simple than the Marshallian

[1] The graph would be similar to Figure 12 even though some of the elasticities were different from those specified, provided they were not sufficiently important to change the signs of the slopes of the lines II or EE.

system of curves because the latter uses in the final graphs only
the quantities of each commodity imported and exported. It has
the advantage, however, of not being limited to two commodities.
A further consideration in its favor is its relation to the monetary
mechanisms operative in international trade. The line $\Sigma\Sigma$ expresses the excess $(+)$ of the export values over import values or
the excess $(-)$ of import over export values, i.e., $\sum_{i=1}^{i=n} x_{1i}\phi_{1i}(x_{1i})$, as
a function of the net monetary factor $z_{\frac{1}{2}}$. It is a necessary condition
of the stability of the equilibrium that this line have a negative
slope where it crosses the horizontal axis. For, if the export and
import values do not balance, monetary mechanisms of gold flow
or currency and credit contraction and expansion are set in operation which, if the equilibrium is stable, will make them balance.
Now, if the exports exceed the imports, $\left[\sum_{i=1}^{i=n} x_{1i}\phi_{1i}(x_{1i}) > 0\right]$, these
mechanisms operate to raise the actual schedules of Y_{1k} in coun-
try 1 and depress the actual schedules of Y_{2k} in country 2, or raise
the $c_{\frac{1}{2}}$ exchange rate, i.e., they increase the net monetary factor
$z_{\frac{1}{2}}$. If the above mentioned line is negatively sloped, such a change
in the net monetary factor will cause a decrease in the excess of
exports over imports. If it were positively sloped, the mechanisms
described would simply increase the departure from equilibrium
conditions. Similarly, if the imports exceed the exports for country 1, the monetary processes will decrease $z_{\frac{1}{2}}$ and equilibrium will
be approached if the line representing value of exports minus
value of imports is negatively sloped. The values of exports and
imports to which we have been referring are not, of course, actual
values, but those for fixed-height schedules.

An extension of this graphic method into three dimensions to
accommodate three countries and any number of commodities is
possible. The method of procedure about to be followed could
have been used in the case of two countries but would have been

less satisfactory than that described. Let the equilibrium equations be written in the form (25):

$$
\begin{array}{cccccc}
y_{11}f_{11}(y_{11}) & + & y_{12}f_{12}(y_{12}) & + \cdots + & y_{1n}f_{1n}(y_{1n}) & = 0 \\
+ & & + & & + & \\
y_{11}f_{21}(z_{\frac{1}{2}}y_{11}) & + & y_{12}f_{22}(z_{\frac{1}{2}}y_{12}) & + \cdots + & y_{1n}f_{2n}(z_{\frac{1}{2}}y_{1n}) & = 0 \\
+ & & + & & + & \\
y_{11}f_{31}(z_{\frac{1}{3}}y_{11}) & + & y_{12}f_{32}(z_{\frac{1}{3}}y_{12}) & + \cdots + & y_{1n}f_{3n}(z_{\frac{1}{3}}y_{1n}) & = 0 \\
\| & & \| & & \| & \\
0 & & 0 & & \cdots \quad 0 &
\end{array}
\qquad (89)
$$

The vertical equations allow y_{1k}, and hence $y_{1k}f_{1k}(y_{1k})$ and also $\sum\limits_{i=1}^{i=n} y_{1i}f_{1i}(y_{1i})$ to be expressed as functions of $z_{\frac{1}{2}}$ and $z_{\frac{1}{3}}$.

If $\sum\limits_{i=1}^{i=n} y_{1i}f_{1i}(y_{1i})$ be plotted on the vertical scale against $z_{\frac{1}{2}}$ and $z_{\frac{1}{3}}$ on the two horizontal axes, a surface will be secured. Another surface will be obtained if $\sum\limits_{i=1}^{i=n} y_{1i}f_{2i}(z_{\frac{1}{2}}y_{1i})$ be plotted against $z_{\frac{1}{2}}$ and $z_{\frac{1}{3}}$. The point at which both these surfaces intersect each other and the horizontal plane of the $z_{\frac{1}{2}}$ and $z_{\frac{1}{3}}$ axes will indicate equilibrium.

CHAPTER V

THE EFFECTS OF DISTURBANCES TO EQUILIBRIUM

I. INTRODUCTION

The three preceding chapters provide a mathematical description of the conditions of equilibrium in international trade. It remains to show how such equilibrium is affected by the introduction of a new element or the alteration of one of the previously existing conditions. Specifically, what are the effects on the relative price levels and on the prices of individual commodities resulting from indemnities, loans, duties, bounties, and changes in demand and supply curves?

Most of these phenomena have twofold effects: (*a*) an immediate shift in purchasing power and (*b*) a disruption of the existing balance of indebtedness for the country in question. The proceeds of a duty, a loan, an indemnity, etc., provide additional available funds to be expended in some particular way, and, conversely, the process of obtaining the money for a bounty, a loan, or an indemnity usually involves decreases in the available funds of certain groups. In an extreme case, if the addition to the means of payment resulted in an equal additional expenditure on internationally traded commodities and the decrease in the means of payment in an equal decreased expenditure on such commodities, the disruption of international equilibrium would not occur.[1] But in the typical case the changes in spendable funds also affect domestic commodities. For the sake of simplicity, in developing techniques of analysis we shall temporarily retain the fifth assumption of chapter ii, that the increases or decreases in spend-

[1] Bertil Ohlin, *The Reparations Problem*, Index (Svenska Handelsbanken), No. 28 (April, 1928).

able funds are generally distributed over all commodities in such a way that their net effect is a raising or lowering of all the demand and supply schedules of a country by the same ratio. After the methods of analysis have been developed and applied to the first general case, we shall show that similar results are secured even though this assumption is practically abandoned.

An existing balance of international indebtedness is disrupted by the addition of debits or credits which will, through the mechanisms of adjustment, lead to a new balance. This process of adjustment, involving shifts in the heights of schedules and movements of the price points of commodities along the schedules, may be regarded as independent of the particular character of the debit and credit items introduced, if the changes in the prices and quantities of commodities *directly* affected by the disturbance (e.g., an import duty) be excepted. As concerns these direct effects, each disturbance must be studied individually. As concerns the effects brought about by the mechanism of adjustment, all disturbances are alike (if, as assumed, the changes in spendable funds are generally distributed).

2. TECHNIQUE OF ANALYSIS

The obvious method of investigating the effects of an indemnity, duty, etc., would seem to be (1) to write and solve the equations before the disturbance occurred, (2) to write and solve the equations incorporating the new element, and then (3) to compare the prices on the fixed-height schedules and the relative heights of the schedules, ascertained in (1) and (2), respectively. Unfortunately, this is not usually a practicable procedure. The solution of such non-linear equations even in a relatively simple case is difficult, and in the general case is not feasible.

If, however, some method could be devised which would yield a set of linear equations involving the unknowns, or the changes in the unknowns brought about by the disturbing element, some useful generalizations might be obtained.

Such a procedure is available.[1] Let us take the equations of (22) and (24) for some particular case of equilibrium and introduce into these equations a very small change of the type we wish to study. If it is an indemnity payable from country 2 to country 1, there will appear on the right-hand side of the first equation of (22) a *very small* negative quantity, and on the right-hand side of the second equation of this set a very small positive quantity. All the other equations of (22) and (24) are also to be written. Now, if each equation in the original sets of (22) and (24) be subtracted from the corresponding equations in sets (22) and (24) after the introduction of the indemnity, a new system of equations will be obtained which relate the *changes* of the terms in the original (22) and (24) to the indemnity introduced. If the element of indemnity is very small (and it can be made as small as we choose), it is legitimate to use differentials of the terms in equations (22) and (24), neglecting all product and higher power terms of these differentials. These equations are linear and can be solved for these differentials of y_{1k} and $z_1 \over p$. For sufficiently small disturbances the signs of differentials indicate correctly the direction of change, plus or minus, in the unknowns y_{1k} and $z_1 \over p$. Let us assume that we know the correct y_{1k} and $z_1 \over p$ values after a very small element of indemnity has been introduced. We then introduce a second very small additional indemnity and again ascertain the signs of the differentials. Thus we may proceed by successive steps until the very small elements of indemnity total to the required amount. If, throughout the process, the differentials of the unknowns always have the same respective signs, they in-

[1] This method is merely an extension of the device employed so skilfully by A. A. Cournot throughout *Researches into the Mathematical Principles of the Theory of Wealth*. See especially page xv of the "Notes on Cournot's Mathematics" by Irving Fisher and page 57 of the text in the 1927 edition of N. T. Bacon's translation, edited by Irving Fisher.

dicate the signs of the changes in the y_{1k} and $z_{1 \atop p}$ caused by the indemnity.[1]

If all the functions $f_{pk}(y_{pk})$ were linear, we could apply the same
technique at once to calculating the amounts, as well as the signs,
of the changes in the prices and relative heights of the schedules.

We now write the equations involving these differentials as
unknowns. Each term in an equation of (22), before substitution,
was simply $y_{pk}x_{pk}$. The differential of such a term is

$$d(y_{pk}x_{pk}) = x_{pk}dy_{pk} + y_{pk}dx_{pk}$$

$$= x_{pk}\left(1 + \frac{y_{pk}dx_{pk}}{x_{pk}dy_{pk}}\right)dy_{pk}$$

$$= x_{pk}y_{pk}(1 + h_{pk})\frac{dy_{pk}}{y_{pk}} . \tag{90}$$

But since

$$y_{pk} = z_{1 \atop p}y_{1k} , \tag{91}$$

we get

$$d(y_{pk}x_{pk}) = x_{pk}y_{pk}(1 + h_{pk}) \; \frac{z_{1 \atop p}dy_{1k} + y_{1k}dz_{1 \atop p}}{z_{1 \atop p}y_{1k}}$$

$$= x_{pk}y_{pk}(1 + h_{pk})\left[\frac{dy_{1k}}{y_{1k}} + \frac{dz_{1 \atop p}}{z_{1 \atop p}}\right] . \tag{92}$$

We shall hereafter denote the coefficient $x_{pk}y_{pk}(1 + h_{pk})$ by a_{pk}.

$$a_{pk} = x_{pk}y_{pk}(1 + h_{pk}) . \tag{93}$$

[1] We may infer that each differential has a constant sign through the successive
steps if the coefficients for the successive solutions always conform to the appropriate
criterion. The criterion might require all import demands to be elastic and all
export supply elasticities to be positive. If the various elasticities conformed to this
criterion throughout the ranges of variation of the prices from the old to the new
equilibrium, any conclusion which could be deduced from the criterion regarding the
sign of the differentials would obviously hold for every step.

For an imported commodity, $a_{pk} \gtrless 0$ according as $h_{pk} \gtrless -1$. For an exported commodity, $a_{pk} \gtrless 0$ as $h_{pk} \gtrless -1$. Excluding a case which rarely if ever occurs, in which $0 > h_{pk} > -1$, i.e., in which the total value of exports is a decreasing function of quantity exported, we may say the a_{pk} for exports is positive if the export supply curve is positively sloped, but negative if that curve is negatively sloped.

The equations involving the differentials of the terms of the equation (22) may now be set down. Let there be an indemnity I payable by country 2 to country 1, measured in the money of country 1. Let dI represent a very small element of this indemnity. We then have the m equations:

$$a_{11}\frac{dy_{11}}{y_{11}} + \cdots + a_{1n}\frac{dy_{1n}}{y_{1n}} \qquad\qquad = \frac{-dI}{r_1}.$$

$$a_{21}\frac{dy_{11}}{y_{11}} + \cdots + a_{2n}\frac{dy_{1n}}{y_{1n}} + \left[\sum_{i=1}^{i=n} a_{2i}\right]\frac{dz_1}{\dfrac{2}{z_1}}{\dfrac{}{2}} = \frac{(+dI)z_{\frac{1}{2}}}{r_1}.$$

$$a_{31}\frac{dy_{11}}{y_{11}} + \cdots + a_{3n}\frac{dy_{1n}}{y_{1n}} + \left[\sum_{i=1}^{i=n} a_{3i}\right]\frac{dz_{\frac{1}{3}}}{z_{\frac{1}{3}}} = 0. \qquad (94)$$

$$\cdots \cdots \cdots \cdots \cdots \cdots \cdots$$

$$a_{m1}\frac{dy_{11}}{y_{11}} + \cdots + a_{mn}\frac{dy_{1n}}{y_{1n}} + \qquad \left[\sum_{i=1}^{i=n} a_{mi}\right]\frac{dz_{\frac{1}{m}}}{z_{\frac{1}{m}}} = 0.$$

In these equations the a_{pk}'s are to be regarded as coefficients and the $\dfrac{dy_{1k}}{y_{1k}}$'s and the $\dfrac{dz_{\frac{1}{p}}}{z_{\frac{1}{p}}}$'s as the unknowns. Obviously, $\dfrac{-dI}{r_1}$ is some very small negative value and $\dfrac{(+dI)\,z_{\frac{1}{2}}}{r_1}$ some very small positive value.

Each term in the equations of (24) was, before substitution, simply x_{pk}, and its differential would be dx_{pk}. But this may be written

$$dx_{pk} = x_{pk} \frac{y_{pk}}{x_{pk}} \frac{dx_{pk}}{dy_{pk}} \frac{dy_{pk}}{y_{pk}}$$

$$= x_{pk} h_{pk} \frac{dy_{pk}}{y_{pk}} . \tag{95}$$

We shall hereafter denote $x_{pk}h_{pk}$ by b_{pk}.

$$b_{pk} = x_{pk} h_{pk} . \tag{96}$$

$$dx_{pk} = b_{pk} \frac{dy_{pk}}{y_{pk}} = b_{pk} \left(\frac{dy_{1k}}{y_{1k}} + \frac{\frac{dz_1}{p}}{\frac{z_1}{p}} \right) . \tag{97}$$

For commodities imported, x_{pk} and h_{pk} are both negative; and b_{pk} is therefore positive. For commodities exported, b_{pk} takes the sign of h_{pk}, i.e., b_{pk} is positive for positively sloped supply curves and negative for negatively sloped supply curves.[1]

The n equations derived by taking the differentials of the terms of the equations (24) are then:

$$\left(b_{11} + \sum_{i=2}^{i=m} b_{i1} \right) \frac{dy_{11}}{y_{11}} \qquad + b_{21} \frac{\frac{dz_1}{2}}{\frac{z_1}{2}} + \cdots + b_{m1} \frac{\frac{dz_1}{m}}{\frac{z_1}{m}} = 0 .$$

$$\left(b_{12} + \sum_{i=2}^{i=m} b_{i2} \right) \frac{dy_{12}}{y_{12}} \qquad + b_{22} \frac{\frac{dz_1}{2}}{\frac{z_1}{2}} + \cdots + b_{m2} \frac{\frac{dz_1}{m}}{\frac{z_1}{m}} = 0 . \tag{98}$$

$$\cdots \cdots \cdots \cdots \cdots \cdots \cdots \cdots \cdots$$

$$\left(b_{1n} + \sum_{i=2}^{i=m} b_{in} \right) \frac{dy_{1n}}{y_{1n}} + b_{2n} \frac{\frac{dz_1}{2}}{\frac{z_1}{2}} + \cdots + b_{mn} \frac{\frac{dz_1}{m}}{\frac{z_1}{m}} = 0 .$$

[1] If the supply curve is horizontal and dy_{pk} is consequently zero, neither the a_{pk} nor the b_{pk} coefficients can be used, since they involve a division by dy_{pk}.

The analysis of this case is deferred to a later portion of this chapter.

$$
\begin{array}{|ccccc|ccccc|c|}
\hline
\dfrac{dz_1}{z_1}\dfrac{2}{2} & \dfrac{dz_1}{z_1}\dfrac{3}{3} & \dfrac{dz_1}{z_1}\dfrac{4}{4} & \cdots & \dfrac{dz_1}{z_1}\dfrac{m}{m} & \dfrac{dy_{11}}{y_{11}} & \dfrac{dy_{12}}{y_{12}} & \dfrac{dy_{13}}{y_{13}} & \cdots & \dfrac{dy_{1n}}{y_{1n}} & \dfrac{(+dI)z_1}{r_1}\dfrac{2}{\;} \\
\hline
\sum_1^n a_{2i} & 0 & 0 & \cdots & 0 & a_{21} & a_{22} & a_{23} & \cdots & a_{2n} & r_1 \\
0 & \sum_1^n a_{3i} & 0 & \cdots & 0 & a_{31} & a_{32} & a_{33} & \cdots & a_{3n} & 0 \\
0 & 0 & \sum_1^n a_{4i} & \cdots & 0 & a_{41} & a_{42} & a_{43} & \cdots & a_{4n} & 0 \\
\vdots & \vdots & \vdots & \vdots & \vdots & \vdots & \vdots & \vdots & \vdots & \vdots & \vdots \\
0 & 0 & 0 & \cdots & \sum_1^n a_{mi} & a_{m1} & a_{m2} & a_{m3} & \cdots & a_{mn} & 0 \\
b_{21} & b_{31} & b_{41} & \cdots & b_{m1} & \left(b_{11}+\sum_2^m b_{i1}\right) & 0 & 0 & \cdots & 0 & 0 \\
b_{22} & b_{32} & b_{42} & \cdots & b_{m2} & 0 & \left(b_{12}+\sum_2^m b_{i2}\right) & 0 & \cdots & 0 & 0 \\
b_{23} & b_{33} & b_{43} & \cdots & b_{m3} & 0 & 0 & \left(b_{13}+\sum_2^m b_{i3}\right) & \cdots & 0 & 0 \\
\vdots & \vdots & \vdots & \vdots & \vdots & \vdots & \vdots & \vdots & \vdots & \vdots & \vdots \\
b_{2n} & b_{3n} & b_{4n} & \cdots & b_{mn} & 0 & 0 & 0 & \cdots & \left(b_{1n}+\sum_2^m b_{in}\right) & 0 \\
\hline
\end{array}
\tag{99}
$$

In the $(m+n)$ equations of (94) and (98) there are $(m-1)$ unknowns, $\dfrac{\frac{dz_1}{p}}{\frac{z_1}{p}}$, and n unknowns, $\dfrac{dy_{1k}}{y_{1k}}$, or $(m+n-1)$ unknowns. But since one of the equations of (22) and (24) can always be derived from the $(m+n-1)$ others, and since the equations of (94) and (98) can be obtained by subtracting the respective equations of two sets of (22) and (24), any one of the equations of (94) and (98) is derivable from the other $(m+n-1)$ and may be omitted.

We next arrange the equations of (94), omitting the first, and those of (98) in such a formation, (99), that the theorems of Appendix I may be applied. The unknowns are written above the horizontal line and the coefficients of these unknowns directly beneath. To the extreme right are the terms on the right-hand side of the equation. Beneath the horizontal ruling there appear in the first $(m-1)$ rows the equations 2 to m of (94), and in the last n rows the n equations of (98).

3. EFFECTS OF DISTURBANCES IN THE GENERAL CASE

We may consider first the case in which every a and every b is positive. This implies that every import demand is elastic and every export supply curve has a positive slope (positive elasticity). For convenience we shall designate this as the "normal" case and these elasticities as "normal elasticities." In Appendix I, section 2, it is demonstrated for such a case that the unknowns of which the individual a's are the coefficients, i.e., the $\dfrac{dy_{1k}}{y_{1k}}$'s, are of opposite sign from the constant terms, and that the unknowns of which the individual b's are the coefficients, i.e., the $\dfrac{\frac{dz_1}{p}}{\frac{z_1}{p}}$'s, are of the same sign as the constant terms. In equations (99) representing the effects of an indemnity paid by country 2 to country 1 the constant term, $\dfrac{(+dI)z_{\frac{1}{2}}}{r_1}$, is positive; hence all the $\dfrac{dy_{1k}}{y_{1k}}$'s are negative

and the $\dfrac{dz_1}{z_1}$'s positive. In other words, the fixed-height schedule
prices of both imports and exports in the country receiving the
indemnity decrease, but the height of the schedules in this country (assuming the exchange rate is constant) increases relative to
those of every other country.

If we let the indemnity-paying country be country 1, the constant term in (99) is negative, and we find by similar analysis that
the fixed-height schedule prices of imports and exports of the indemnity-paying country rise, but that the height of its schedules
decreases relative to those of every other country.

Now

$$\frac{dy_{2k}}{y_{2k}} = \frac{dy_{1k}}{y_{1k}} + \frac{dz_{\frac{1}{2}}}{z_{\frac{1}{2}}} . \tag{100}$$

If countries 1 and 2 be regarded as the receiving and paying countries, respectively, we know from the preceding analysis that
$\dfrac{dy_{2k}}{y_{2k}}$ is of different sign from $\dfrac{dy_{1k}}{y_{1k}}$ but of the same sign as $\dfrac{dz_{\frac{1}{2}}}{z_{\frac{1}{2}}}$.
Therefore, as between the indemnity-paying and the indemnity-
receiving countries the proportionate change in the net monetary
factor, or, with the exchange rate constant, the proportionate
change in the relative height of the two countries' schedules, is
greater than the proportionate change in any export or import
fixed-height schedule price. Consequently, in this "normal" case
no actual money import or export price can rise as much as the
domestic price level of the indemnity-receiving country or fall as
much as the domestic price level of the indemnity-paying country.

From the behavior of the fixed-height schedule prices it is readily inferred that for country 1 receiving the indemnity, the quan-

tity of each import increases and the quantity of each export decreases. For country 2 the quantity of each export increases and the quantity of each import decreases.

All these conclusions for the "normal" case are conveniently summarized in Table I. Country 3 is typical of any country 3 to m.

TABLE I

EFFECTS OF AN INDEMNITY PAID BY COUNTRY 2 TO COUNTRY 1

	SIGNS OF CHANGES IN:				
COUNTRIES	Net Monetary Factor, $\dfrac{z_1}{p}$, for Country p	Import Prices on Fixed-Height Schedules	Export Prices on Fixed-Height Schedules	Quantities Imported	Quantities Exported
1		−	−	+	−
2	+	+	+	−	+
3	+	?	?	?	?

$$\frac{dz_{\frac{2}{3}}}{z_{\frac{2}{3}}} < 0. \qquad \frac{dz_{\frac{1}{2}}}{z_{\frac{1}{2}}} > -\frac{dy_{1k}}{y_{1k}} \text{ or } \frac{dy_{2k}}{y_{2k}}.$$

In the following section it will be shown that these tabulated results are not dependent on the assumption of equal relative shifts in all the schedules of a country.

Much has been said recently concerning the necessity or lack of necessity of changes in prices to accomplish international transfers such as reparations. In this problem the greatest care must be exercised to distinguish the factors which affect both domestic commodity prices and internationally traded commodity prices from those which are peculiar to the latter. Both groups of prices are affected by monetary causes which move the demand and supply schedules up or down. But when the demand or supply schedules of a country for internationally traded goods are shifted by monetary changes, they stand in different relations to the schedules of other countries. In general, if the supply curves are positively sloped, the equilibrium price points tend to move along the schedules in such a way as to compensate for the monetary shift of the schedules. Thus, it is quite conceivable, especially if the indemnity paying and receiving countries are of approximately equal size, that there might be relatively minor changes in the prices of internationally traded commodities. As regards domestic prices, the situation is different. These prices also reflect monetary changes peculiar to the country, but without the compensation resulting from the schedules being related to foreign-country schedules. Such compensation as occurs comes from competition between the domestic and the import and export products, i.e., from the fact that domestic products are not purely domestic. It is not, therefore, legitimate to conclude that price changes of all commodities will be small because the price changes of internationally traded commodities are expected to be small.

Our conclusions regarding the effect of an indemnity on the fixed-schedule prices and the relative heights of price levels were based on "normal" elasticities. Even if some of the elasticities were exceptional, we should expect the signs of the differentials to remain unchanged in many cases (but not the sign of the differential of the price on a fixed-schedule supply curve of negative slope[1]), particularly if the commodity imports or exports of exceptional elasticities did not make up a large portion of the trade in a commodity, or a large portion of the trade of more than one country. One might view the problem in terms of Marshall's "bales." Although some of the elasticities of individual commodities may be exceptional, the elasticity for the composite bale may still be of the "normal" type. Further, we shall see, when we analyze the two-country, two-commodity case, that the signs of the changes in the fixed-height schedule prices (excepting prices on negatively sloped export supply curves), in the quantities imported and exported, and in the net monetary factor are for wide ranges of exceptional elasticities the same as for the "normal" case.

The preceding discussion of the effects of an indemnity applies also to the extension of loans, the repayment of loans, immigrant

[1] See Cases IV–VIII for two countries discussed later in this chapter.

remittances, gifts, and any other additional remittance appearing in the international balances.

A duty or bounty may be studied either by specific mathematical analysis, i.e., by introducing a very small element of duty or bounty and analyzing its effects upon the differentials of the prices and of the net monetary factors, or else by considering the disturbance to the equation of international indebtedness caused by the duty or bounty. The former method gives a complete solution since it incorporates the changes in the prices and quantities of the commodities directly affected. But since it involves difficulties which would require extended treatment, and since the alternative procedure yields exactly the same general conclusions, we shall adopt this simpler method of approach.

The imposition of a duty on any import operates directly to reduce the net price paid to foreigners and to decrease the quantity imported. Consequently, the foreign countries exporting the product lose a portion of their means of payment for their imports and must increase the value of their exports relative to that of their imports. They are in a position analogous to that of the indemnity-paying country. On the other hand, the country levying the duty must increase the value of its imports relative to the value of its exports; it takes the rôle of the indemnity-receiving country. Thus all the reactions we have described for the indemnity-receiving or the borrowing country will occur in the country which levies the import duties. But the statement that import prices on the fixed-height schedules will decrease does not, of course, apply to the commodities on which the duty has been imposed.

It is interesting to observe that the argument for the tariff as a cause of prosperity may have a certain limited significance. A major tariff increase will tend to raise the domestic price level and thus may initiate a prosperity phase of the business cycle. Conversely, a large increase in foreign import duties affecting a considerable portion of the exports of a country will tend to depress domestic prices.

Except for the fact that the proceeds of a tax are again expended, the effects of an import duty are exactly duplicated by a decrease in import demand, i.e., a lowering of the schedule of import demand. An increase in import demand, conversely, would have general effects analogous to the payment of an indemnity.

The results of a rise in export supply schedules and of export duties are alike, except as regards the expenditure of the duty. Either of these disturbances decreases or increases the value of exports according as the foreign demand for them is elastic or inelastic. In the former case they operate like the payment, in the latter case like the receipt, of indemnities as regards their general effects. Export bounties and a lowering of the export supply schedule are analogous, except for the effects of securing the bounty funds. If the foreign demand for the commodities in question is elastic, these disturbances operate as would the receipt of an indemnity; if not, they operate as would the payment of an indemnity.

4. EXTENSION OF THE TECHNIQUE OF ANALYSIS

The results of the preceding section indicating the effects of a disturbance to international equilibrium are valid beyond the limits of the assumptions from which they were derived.

Thus far we have assumed that all the schedules in a country shift up or down by the same ratio, i.e., that r_p is the same for all commodities in any country p. We were thus able to define the net monetary factor, $z_{\frac{1}{p}}$, also the same for all commodities, by equation (10),

$$z_{\frac{1}{p}} = \frac{r_1}{r_p}\, c_{\frac{1}{p}}\,. \tag{10}$$

Let us now consider the case in which the relative changes in the heights of the various schedules are not of uniform magnitude. Under such conditions there must be a separate r_{pk} for each commodity (identified by the additional commodity subscript). Furthermore, $z_{\frac{1}{p}k}$, which relates the schedules of country p to those of country 1, must also vary from commodity to commodity.

$$z_{\frac{1}{p}k} = \frac{r_{1k}}{r_{pk}}\, c_{\frac{1}{p}}. \tag{100a}$$

Very small relative changes in $z_{\frac{1}{p}k}$ may be written:

$$\frac{dz_{\frac{1}{p}k}}{z_{\frac{1}{p}k}} = \frac{dr_{1k}}{r_{1k}} - \frac{dr_{pk}}{r_{pk}} + \frac{dc_{\frac{1}{p}}}{c_{\frac{1}{p}}}. \tag{100b}$$

Now, if $\dfrac{dz_{\frac{1}{p}k}}{z_{\frac{1}{p}k}}$ is of the same sign but of different magnitude for commodities $1, 2, \ldots, n$, as regards the countries 1 and p, it can be shown that the effects of an indemnity in the general normal case are similar to those tabulated in the preceding section. It is important, therefore, to inquire into the conditions which will lead to $\dfrac{dz_{\frac{1}{p}k}}{z_{\frac{1}{p}k}}$'s of this type.

With convertible currencies and a constant exchange rate, which may be assumed for convenience in the discussion, equation $(100b)$ becomes

$$\frac{dz_{\frac{1}{p}k}}{z_{\frac{1}{p}k}} = \frac{dr_{1k}}{r_{1k}} - \frac{dr_{pk}}{r_{pk}}. \tag{100c}$$

The effect of a disturbance, such as an indemnity, is either to lower or to raise the schedules of a country. This leads to the requirement that $\dfrac{dr_{pk}}{r_{pk}}$ be of the same sign, i.e., $\geqq 0$ or $\leqq 0$, for all commodities ($k = 1, 2, \ldots, n$) in any country p. From $(100c)$ it is evident that the sign of $\dfrac{dz_{\frac{1}{p}k}}{z_{\frac{1}{p}k}}$ is uniform, first, if $\dfrac{dr_{1k}}{r_{1k}}$ and $\dfrac{dr_{pk}}{r_{pk}}$

are of different signs, or second, if either is consistently larger or smaller in absolute magnitude than the other. The first of these conditions obtains whenever a disturbance to equilibrium, such as an indemnity or loan, increases the spendable funds in one country and decreases them in the other (countries 1 and 2 in the case in the preceding section). The second of these conditions usually exists whenever there is a direct increase or decrease in the spendable funds in one country but only a minor change in the spendable funds in the other country, secondary to and resulting from the disturbance in which the country is not directly involved (e.g., countries 1 and 3 or countries 2 and 3 in the cases in the preceding section). Instances in which the secondary effects are so concentrated on one or two particular commodities as to cause large relative changes in the heights of their schedules would be possible but probably exceptional.

We may now proceed to show that the effects of an indemnity, loan, etc., are not altered by introducing variations in the magnitude (but not the sign) of $\dfrac{dz_{1_k}/p}{z_{1_k}/p}$ for different commodities.

By selecting a set of positive multipliers, λ, such that $\lambda_{\frac{1}{p}_k}$ is inversely proportional to $\dfrac{dz_{1_k}/p}{z_{1_k}/p}$ for $k = 1, 2, \ldots, n$, we get

$$\lambda_{\frac{1}{p}_1}\frac{dz_{1_1}/p}{z_{1_1}/p} = \lambda_{\frac{1}{p}_2}\frac{dz_{1_2}/p}{z_{1_2}/p} = \cdots = \lambda_{\frac{1}{p}_n}\frac{dz_{1_n}/p}{z_{1_n}/p}. \qquad (100d)$$

In case any $\dfrac{dz_{1_k}/p}{z_{1_k}/p}$ is zero, the $\lambda_{\frac{1}{p}_k}$ may be regarded as infinite. By substituting $\dfrac{1}{\lambda_{\frac{1}{p}_k}}\left[\lambda_{\frac{1}{p}_k}\dfrac{dz_{1_k}/p}{z_{1_k}/p}\right]$ for $\dfrac{dz_{1_k}/p}{z_{1_k}/p}$ and treating $\dfrac{1}{\lambda_{\frac{1}{p}_k}}$ as part of the coefficient and $\left[\lambda_{\frac{1}{p}k}\dfrac{dz_{\frac{1}{p}k}}{z_{\frac{1}{p}k}}\right]$ as the unknown, we may use the methods

of analysis already developed in this chapter. For $\left[\lambda_{\frac{1}{p}k}\dfrac{dz_{\frac{1}{p}k}}{z_{\frac{1}{p}k}}\right]$ is now

an unknown similar to $\dfrac{dz_{\frac{1}{p}}}{z_{\frac{1}{p}}}$, the same for all commodities, and the

multiplication of the coefficients of the $\dfrac{dz_{\frac{1}{p}k}}{z_{\frac{1}{p}k}}$'s by the positive $\dfrac{1}{\lambda_{\frac{1}{p}k}}$'s

does not cause any reversal of sign. The vanishing of some of the
coefficients when their $\lambda_{\frac{1}{p}k}$'s are infinite does not change the type
of the determinant.

Since the essential characteristics of the set of equations (99)
are not altered by these processes, the results are strictly parallel

with those obtained in the original solution. The $\dfrac{dy_{pk}}{y_{pk}}$'s have the

same signs as before. Each $\left[\lambda_{\frac{1}{p}k}\dfrac{dz_{\frac{1}{p}k}}{z_{\frac{1}{p}k}}\right]$ is of the same sign as the

$\dfrac{dz_{\frac{1}{p}}}{z_{\frac{1}{p}}}$ in the previous solution. And, since $\lambda_{\frac{1}{p}k}$ is positive, the $\dfrac{dz_{\frac{1}{p}k}}{z_{\frac{1}{p}k}}$'s

for the various commodities ($k = 1, 2, \ldots, n$) have the same

sign as the corresponding $\dfrac{dz_{\frac{1}{p}}}{z_{\frac{1}{p}}}$.

It should be observed, however, that any statement based on
the relation in equation (100) must of course be made relative to

the $\dfrac{dz_{\frac{1}{p}k}}{z_{\frac{1}{p}k}}$ for the particular commodity.

We come now to the second stage in the generalization of our conclusions. Let us assume that in reaction to a disturbance of international equilibrium the schedules of a country shift up (or down) by varying relative amounts and that they also change their shapes. For our purposes it will be convenient to regard such adjustments as occurring in two distinct steps.

Arbitrarily, we may imagine that the changes in shape occurred just before the disturbance and that these changes left all the import demand and export supply curves still passing through their previous equilibrium points. Obviously, this would cause no alteration in the existing equilibrium; prices and quantities would remain the same. Then the adjustment to the disturbance in international equilibrium could be regarded as taking place through upward (or downward) relative shifts of these schedules. But, as we have seen, this latter type of adjustment leads to uniform signs of $\dfrac{dz_{1}}{\frac{-}{p}}_{k} \Big/ \dfrac{z_{1}}{\frac{-}{p}}_{k}$ for pairs of countries which are oppositely affected by the disturbance and usually also for pairs of countries which are affected primarily and secondarily by the disturbance. And if the $\dfrac{dz_{1}}{\frac{-}{p}}_{k} \Big/ \dfrac{z_{1}}{\frac{-}{p}}_{k}$'s are uniform in sign for $k = 1, 2, \ldots, n$, the results are exactly parallel to those in the original case.

Nor can legitimate objection be raised to this separation of the adjustment process into two parts, one of which is conceived of as preceding the disturbance. For it is a sufficient answer to any such objection that the final equilibrium is dependent only on the final shape and height of the schedules and not on the sequence of change leading to them.

In this connection it is important to note that the coefficients in the set of equations (99) would be derived from the changed schedules. Consequently the type to which any case belongs depends on the elasticity of the new schedules.

In the discussion of subsequent cases we shall not repeat this process of generalizing our conclusions. Although such conclusions will be derived from the original assumption of the uniformity in the relative shifts of all the schedules in a country, they may, by the processes just described, be extended to cover the cases in which the relative shifts are non-uniform in magnitude, although uniform in direction, and in which the schedules experience changes of shape.

5. PROCEDURE FOR CASES INVOLVING CONSTANT COSTS

The a_{pk} and b_{pk} elements in the determinant cannot be used for an export with a horizontal supply curve. In such a supply curve

$$y_{pk} = K_{pk} .\tag{101}$$

in which K_{pk} is some constant.

In place of (90) we write

$$d(x_{pk}y_{pk}) = y_{pk}dx_{pk} ;\tag{102}$$

and instead of (97) we use simply dx_{pk}. Now dx_{pk} is an additional unknown. But from the other remaining unknowns one can be eliminated, for

$$dy_{pk} = 0 .\tag{103}$$

$$dy_{pk} = d\left(z_{1}y_{1k}\right) = \frac{dy_{1k}}{y_{1k}} + \frac{\frac{dz_{1}}{p}}{\frac{z_{1}}{p}} = 0 .\tag{104}$$

$$-\frac{dy_{1k}}{y_{1k}} = \frac{\frac{dz_{1}}{p}}{\frac{z_{1}}{p}} .\tag{105}$$

In each equation the coefficients of $\dfrac{dy_{1k}}{y_{1k}}$ may be combined with those of $\dfrac{\frac{dz_{1}}{p}}{\frac{z_{1}}{p}}$, after changing the sign of the former, thereby eliminating the variable $\dfrac{dy_{1k}}{y_{1k}}$. The determinant solution of any such set of equations is then readily accomplished. It is interesting to observe that if two countries, say countries 2 and 3, are both exporting, and after the disturbance continue to export, a commodity whose supply curve in each country is horizontal, the changes in the net monetary factors relating the respective countries to country 1 are equal. This means that the change in the net monetary factor connecting countries 2 and 3 is zero.

$$-\frac{dy_{1k}}{y_{1k}} = \frac{dz_{\frac{1}{2}}}{z_{\frac{1}{2}}} \, . \tag{106}$$

$$-\frac{dy_{1k}}{y_{1k}} = \frac{dz_{\frac{1}{3}}}{z_{\frac{1}{3}}} \, . \tag{107}$$

$$\frac{dz_{\frac{1}{2}}}{z_{\frac{1}{2}}} = \frac{dz_{\frac{1}{3}}}{z_{\frac{1}{3}}} \, . \tag{108}$$

As a practical matter, the failure of the a's and b's, and hence the typical determinant solution, is not very serious. If, instead of an exactly horizontal line, one very nearly horizontal is utilized, the error in the solution will be small. If the same signs for the differentials are obtained whether the slope be positive or negative, there is reasonable assurance (assuming continuity) that the signs of the results for the constant cost case are then known. If the sign of a differential changes as the slope changes from positive to negative, the differential (assuming its continuity) will be zero for the horizontal curve.

6. STABILITY OF EQUILIBRIUM

The conditions for equilibrium in international trade are of two types: (a) equilibrium within each industry, and (b) equilibrium as regards the monetary mechanism of international trade. For (a) it is primarily necessary that differential income be equal to differential cost for each business enterprise and that total income at least equal total cost for each business enterprise. This would eliminate negatively sloped supply curves, except such as result from economies of large-scale output for the industry which cannot be advantageously appropriated by a particular business enterprise or combination of enterprises.

For (b) it is fundamentally necessary that the changes in the relative heights of the schedules of the respective countries which result from any disturbance to the equality of international indebtedness shall lead to a restoration of that equality. This may be tested to some extent in specific cases by comparing the sign of the $\dfrac{dz_1}{p}\Big/\dfrac{z_1}{p}$ obtained from the equations with the sign which would result from the monetary mechanisms in operation. Thus, if an indemnity is paid by country 2 to country 1, we know that the monetary changes will elevate the heights of the schedules in country 1 relative to those in country 2 (assuming the exchange rate is constant). This means that $dz_{\frac{1}{2}}$, and hence $\dfrac{dz_{\frac{1}{2}}}{z_{\frac{1}{2}}}$, is positive.

For the equilibrium to be stable, $\dfrac{dz_{\frac{1}{2}}}{z_{\frac{1}{2}}}$, as calculated from our equations, must also be positive. If it were of opposite sign, the monetary mechanisms which are operative would not re-establish but would still further unbalance the equation of international indebtedness.

7. THE TWO-COUNTRY, TWO-COMMODITY CASES WITH VARIOUS ELASTICITIES

a) *Statement and Solution of Cases:* A detailed solution of the two-country, two-commodity case for the effect of a disturbance to the balance of international indebtedness will illustrate some of our preceding statements and will afford a further basis for generalization regarding the effects of such disturbances upon the terms of trade and the behavior of sectional price levels. Let the disturbance be any additional remittance payable by country 2 to country 1, such as an indemnity, loan, etc. We shall use the term "indemnity" as typical of such disturbances. The equations and the determinant Δ_{11}[1] for their solution, following the schematic arrangement in (99) but with a substitution of dI' for $\dfrac{(dI)z_{\frac{1}{2}}}{r_1}$, are:

$$
\begin{array}{ccc}
\dfrac{dz_{\frac{1}{2}}}{z_{\frac{1}{2}}} & \dfrac{dy_{11}}{y_{11}} & \dfrac{dy_{12}}{y_{12}}
\end{array}
$$

$$
\left|
\begin{array}{ccc}
(a_{21}+a_{22}) & a_{21} & a_{22} \\
b_{21} & (b_{11}+b_{21}) & 0 \\
b_{22} & 0 & (b_{12}+b_{22})
\end{array}
\right|
\begin{array}{c}
+dI' \\
0 \\
0
\end{array}
\qquad (109)
$$

The solutions for the unknowns are easily written.

$$
\frac{dz_{\frac{1}{2}}}{z_{\frac{1}{2}}} = +\frac{(+dI')(b_{11}+b_{21})(b_{12}+b_{22})}{\Delta_{11}} . \tag{110}
$$

$$
\frac{dy_{11}}{y_{11}} = -\frac{(+dI')b_{21}(b_{12}+b_{22})}{\Delta_{11}} . \tag{111}
$$

$$
\frac{dy_{12}}{y_{12}} = -\frac{(+dI')(b_{11}+b_{21})(b_{22})}{\Delta_{11}} . \tag{112}
$$

$$
\Delta_{11} = (a_{21}+a_{22})(b_{11}+b_{21})(b_{12}+b_{22}) - a_{21}b_{21}(b_{12}+b_{22}) - a_{22}(b_{11}+b_{21})b_{22} .
$$

$$
= a_{21}b_{11}(b_{12}+b_{22}) + a_{22}(b_{11}+b_{21})b_{12} . \tag{113}
$$

---

[1] This is called Δ_{11} because the rows and columns are numbered beginning with 2.

From (100), (110), (111), and (112),

$$\frac{dy_{21}}{y_{21}} = \frac{dz_{\frac{1}{2}}}{z_{\frac{1}{2}}} + \frac{dy_{11}}{y_{11}} = +\frac{(+dI')b_{11}(b_{12}+b_{22})}{\Delta_{11}} . \tag{114}$$

$$\frac{dy_{22}}{y_{22}} = \frac{dz_{\frac{1}{2}}}{z_{\frac{1}{2}}} + \frac{dy_{12}}{y_{12}} = +\frac{(+dI')(b_{11}+b_{21})b_{12}}{\Delta_{11}} . \tag{115}$$

We shall distinguish twelve cases, for the first eight of which the determinant and general solutions of (109) to (115) can be used. A special solution is necessary for Cases IX–XII. The disturbance to equilibrium is, as stated, an additional remittance, such as an indemnity which must be paid by country 2 to country 1. Commodity 1 is an import for country 1 and an export for country 2; commodity 2 is an export for country 1 and an import for country 2.

Case I.—Normal case. Both import demands are elastic, and both export supply curves are positively sloped. Therefore every a and b is positive.

Case II.—One import demand is elastic and one inelastic; both export supply curves are positively sloped. Either a_{11} or a_{22} is negative; the other a's and b's are positive.

Case III.—Both import demands are inelastic; both export supply curves are positively sloped. a_{11} and a_{22} are negative; a_{12} and a_{21}, and all the b's, are positive.

Case IV.—Both import demands are elastic; the export supply of country 1 for commodity 2 is negatively sloped, subject to the arbitrary limitation that $|h_{12}| > |h_{22}|$. The other export supply curve is positively sloped. a_{12} and b_{12} are negative; the other a's and b's are positive. $(b_{12}+b_{22})$ is negative.

Case V.—Both import demands are elastic; the export supply of country 2 for commodity 1 is negatively sloped, subject to the limitation, $|h_{21}| > |h_{11}|$. The other export supply is positively sloped. a_{21} and b_{21} are negative. The other a's and b's are positive. $(b_{11}+b_{21})$ is negative.

Case VI.—Both import demands are elastic; both export supply curves are negatively sloped but subject to the restrictions that $|h_{12}| > |h_{22}|$ and $|h_{21}| > |h_{11}|$. a_{12}, a_{21}, b_{12}, b_{21}, $(b_{12}+b_{22})$, and $(b_{11}+b_{21})$ are all negative. a_{11}, a_{22}, b_{11}, and b_{22} are positive.

Case VII.—A consideration of the effects on cases IV, V, and VI of allowing either a_{11} or a_{22} to be negative, i.e., allowing one of the import demands to be inelastic.

Case VIII.—A consideration of the effects on Cases IV, V, and VI of allowing both a_{11} and a_{22} to be negative, i.e., both import demands to be inelastic.

Case IX.—Both import demands are elastic; one export supply curve, of commodity 2 by country 1, is of zero slope, and the other is positively sloped. a_{12} and b_{12} drop out; the other a's and b's are positive.

Case X.—Both import demands are elastic; one export supply curve, of commodity 1 by country 2, is of zero slope, and the other is positively sloped. a_{21} and b_{21} drop out; the other a's and b's are positive.

Case XI.—Both import demands are elastic; both export supply curves are horizontal. a_{12}, b_{12}, a_{21}, and b_{21} drop out. a_{11}, b_{11}, a_{22}, and b_{22} are positive.

Case XII.—A consideration of the effects on Cases IX, X, and XI of introducing inelastic import demands.

These cases do not, by any means, cover all conceivable combinations, but they are sufficient illustration for our purposes. Table II contains a summary of the solutions.

TABLE II

Effects of an Indemnity Paid by Country 2 to Country 1 with Various Elasticities of Demand and Supply

Signs of—

CASE	$\dfrac{dy_{11}}{y_{11}}$	$\dfrac{dy_{12}}{y_{12}}$	$\dfrac{dz_{\frac{1}{2}}}{z_{\frac{1}{2}}}$	$\dfrac{dy_{21}}{y_{21}}$	$\dfrac{dy_{22}}{y_{22}}$	$(-dx_{11})$ and $(+dx_{21})$	$(+dx_{12})$ and $(-dx_{22})$	Δ_{11}
I.......	−	−	+	+	+	+	−	+
II.......	−	−	+	+	+	+	−	+
III (a) ..	−	−	+	+	+	+	−	+
or (b)...	+	+	−	−	−	−	+	−
IV......	−	+	+	+	+	+	−	−
V.......	−	−	+	−	+	+	−	−
VI......	−	+	+	−	+	+	−	+
IX......	−	∘	+	+	$+$ $=\dfrac{dz_{\frac{1}{2}}}{z_{\frac{1}{2}}}$	+	−	
X.......	$-$ $=-\dfrac{dz_{\frac{1}{2}}}{z_{\frac{1}{2}}}$	−	+	∘	+	+	−	
XI......	$-$ $=-\dfrac{dz_{\frac{1}{2}}}{z_{\frac{1}{2}}}$	∘	+	∘	$+$ $=\dfrac{dz_{\frac{1}{2}}}{z_{\frac{1}{2}}}$	+	−	

VII.....No change in Cases IV, V, and VI.

VIII....Either (a) no change in Cases IV, V, and VI, or
(b) all signs reversed in Cases IV, V, and VI.

XII.....Either (a) no change in Cases IX, X, and XI, or
(b) signs of Cases IX, X, and XI reversed.

Solutions I, IV, V, and VI can be determined from inspection of the general solutions in (110) to (115) and by consideration of the functional relations between y_{pk} and x_{pk}. Solution II is obvious from inspection if a_{11} is negative and a_{22} is positive. If a_{11} is positive and a_{22} is negative, the solution is more difficult. It may be obtained most easily by excluding the equation involving a_{22} and including in its place the equation involving a_{11}. This requires a new solution, but it is simple and the signs of the differentials are then determinable from inspection. Another device which can be used is the reversal of the position of the indemnity receiving and paying countries. Solution III becomes apparent from a consideration of the determinant Δ_{11}. It appears from inspection and trial that if a_{11} and a_{22} are both negative, this determinant may be either positive or negative. In general, it is negative only if a_{11} and a_{22} are based on extremely inelastic demands. For the great majority of cases solution (a) will be found to hold. The results in VII are obtained by a procedure analogous to that described under II, and the results in VIII by a procedure analogous to that in III. In general, solution VIII (b) will hold only for very inelastic demands. In testing the sign of Δ_{11}, it must always be remembered that a_{pk} and b_{pk} are directly related; both involve the same x_{pk} and h_{pk}.[1]

The zeros which appear in solutions IX, X, and XI occur because the y in question is constant on a horizontal supply curve and dy is therefore zero. The equations to be solved for IX are, in the usual formation:

$$
\begin{array}{ccc}
\dfrac{dz_{\frac{1}{2}}}{z_{\frac{1}{2}}} & \dfrac{dy_{11}}{y_{11}} & dx_{12} \\
\end{array}
$$

$$
\left|
\begin{array}{ccc}
(a_{21}+a_{22}) & a_{21} & 0 \\
b_{21} & (b_{11}+b_{21}) & 0 \\
b_{22} & 0 & 1 \\
\end{array}
\right.
\left|
\begin{array}{c}
+(dI') \\
0 \\
0 \\
\end{array}
\right. \tag{116}
$$

The solution gives

$$
\frac{dz_{\frac{1}{2}}}{z_{\frac{1}{2}}} > 0 . \qquad \frac{dy_{11}}{y_{11}} < 0 . \qquad dx_{12} < 0 . \tag{117}
$$

But we also have

$$
\frac{dy_{12}}{y_{12}} = 0 = \frac{dy_{22}}{y_{22}} - \frac{dz_{\frac{1}{2}}}{z_{\frac{1}{2}}} . \tag{118}
$$

[1] In equations (110), (111), (112), (113), (114), and (115), substitution may be made for the a_{pk}'s and b_{pk}'s from (93) and (96) and the expressions then simplified. This relates the differentials directly to the import and export elasticities and facilitates the solution in some of the cases.

Therefore,

$$\frac{dy_{22}}{y_{22}} > 0 . \tag{119}$$

Since $\frac{dy_{11}}{y_{11}} < 0$, the exports of commodity 1 to country 1 from country 2 have increased, $[(-dx_{11}) > 0]$, and this necessitates that $\frac{dy_{21}}{y_{21}} > 0$.

The solutions for X and XI follow the same procedure as IX. The equations for XI are given below.

$$\frac{dy_{12}}{y_{12}} = 0 = \frac{dy_{22}}{y_{22}} - \frac{dz_{\frac{1}{2}}}{z_{\frac{1}{2}}} \quad \text{or} \quad \frac{dy_{22}}{y_{22}} = \frac{dz_{\frac{1}{2}}}{z_{\frac{1}{2}}} . \tag{120}$$

$$\frac{dy_{21}}{y_{21}} = 0 = \frac{dy_{11}}{y_{11}} + \frac{dz_{\frac{1}{2}}}{z_{\frac{1}{2}}} \quad \text{or} \quad \frac{dy_{11}}{y_{11}} = - \frac{dz_{\frac{1}{2}}}{z_{\frac{1}{2}}} . \tag{121}$$

$\dfrac{dz_{\frac{1}{2}}}{z_{\frac{1}{2}}}$	dx_{12}	dx_{21}	
a_{22}	0	y_{21}	$+(dI')$
$-b_{11}$	0	1	0
b_{22}	1	0	0

$$\tag{122}$$

The solution is

$$\frac{dz_{\frac{1}{2}}}{z_{\frac{1}{2}}} = \frac{dy_{22}}{y_{22}} = - \frac{dy_{11}}{y_{11}} = \frac{-(dI')}{-(b_{11}y_{21} + a_{22})} \quad \text{which is} > 0 . \tag{123}$$

$$dx_{12} = \frac{(dI')b_{22}}{-(b_{11}y_{21} + a_{22})} \quad \text{which is} < 0 . \tag{124}$$

$$dx_{21} = \frac{-(dI')b_{11}}{-(b_{11}y_{21} + a_{22})} \quad \text{which is} > 0 . \tag{125}$$

In Case XII the introduction of one inelastic import demand will not change the signs of Cases IX, X, and XI. Two inelastic import demands will not change the signs unless the elasticities be considerably smaller than 1.

A study of these cases will throw some light on the stability of equilibrium in international trade and on the effects of an indemnity or other remittance upon the sectional price levels and the terms of trade.

b) *Stability of Equilibrium:* The monetary mechanisms which are put in operation when an indemnity is to be paid by country 2 to country 1 increase the circulating money media or raise the schedules in country 1 while they decrease the circulating money media or lower the schedules in country 2. This means simply that $z_{\frac{1}{2}}$ increases or that $\dfrac{dz_{\frac{1}{2}}}{z_{\frac{1}{2}}}$ is positive. If the equilibrium is to be stable, the sign of $\dfrac{dz_1}{\frac{z_1}{p}}$ must agree with that deducible from the mechanisms which are known to be operative. Hence, in our cases a positive $\dfrac{dz_{\frac{1}{2}}}{z_{\frac{1}{2}}}$ indicates a stable, and a negative $\dfrac{dz_{\frac{1}{2}}}{z_{\frac{1}{2}}}$ an unstable, equilibrium. The wide range of cases for which the equilibrium is stable in spite of inelastic demands and negatively sloped supply curves—within limits, of course—appears strikingly from Table II. Although the table was constructed deliberately to reflect the important (stable) cases, the ranges within which instability exist are suggested. Generally speaking, instability of equilibrium is due to small negative elasticities of export supply, i.e., export supply curves which have a considerable negative slope, or to import demands of both countries which are highly inelastic. These conditions are not common, however, even for individual commodities, and are highly improbable for a "bale" of exports or of imports composed of many commodities.

c) *Reactions of Sectional Price Levels:* The reactions of sectional price levels to a new item in the balance of international indebtedness are nicely illustrated by the cases. By definition, the payment of an indemnity by country 2 to country 1 in every stable equilibrium case results in a rise of the schedules of country 1 relative to those of country 2. If extraneous influences are barred, the monetary mechanisms will raise the schedules and the domestic price level of country 1 and lower the schedules and domestic price level of country 2.

When the exchange rate is constant, $z_{\frac{1}{2}}$ reflects the height of country 1's schedules relative to those of country 2:

$$z_{\frac{1}{2}} = c_{\frac{1}{2}} \frac{r_1}{r_2}, \tag{126}$$

in which, it will be recalled, r_1 and r_2 are ratios of the heights of the actual money schedules to the fixed-height schedules for the respective countries. Now, if $c_{\frac{1}{2}}$ is constant, the following relation exists between the increments in the terms of equation (126):

$$\Delta \log z_{\frac{1}{2}} = \Delta \log r_1 - \Delta \log r_2 . \tag{127}$$

$\Delta \log r_1$ serves as a measure of the proportionate change in the heights of the schedules and in the domestic price level of country 1. $\Delta \log r_2$ indicates the same for country 2. If the domestic price levels of the two countries move in opposite directions, $\Delta \log r_1$ always has the sign of $\Delta \log z_{\frac{1}{2}}$ and $\Delta \log r_2$ always has the opposite sign.

In the interpretation of the cases in Table II with reference to the behavior of sectional price levels, some assistance may be derived from the definition of the y_{pk}'s by equation (8):

$$\frac{Y_{pk}}{r_p} = y_{pk} . \tag{128}$$

Whence

$$\Delta \frac{Y_{pk}}{r_p} = \Delta y_{pk} . \qquad (129)$$

Obviously, the increments on both sides of (129) are of the same sign. This means simply that if the fixed-schedule or deflated price of a commodity rises (or falls), its actual money price rises (or falls) relative to the domestic price level.

For Cases I, II, and III (a), with positively sloped supply curves, we find that the prices of internationally traded commodities may have risen or fallen, but they did not rise proportionately as much as the price level of country 1 or fall as much as the price level of country 2. The absolute rise or fall of international prices depends on the various elasticities and on all the monetary elements governing inflation and deflation in the respective countries.

From Cases IX, X, and XI, it is evident that if an export has a horizontal supply curve the money price at which it is supplied varies proportionately with the domestic price level of the country exporting it.

Cases IV, V, VI, VII, and VIII (a) show that, if the export supply curve is negatively sloped for the country receiving the indemnity, the price of the export rises relatively above the height of the domestic price level, which in turn has experienced an absolute rise. But if the indemnity-paying country is supplying a decreasing cost commodity, then its price falls relatively below the domestic price level, which has in turn suffered an absolute decline.

The behavior of export and import price levels relative to the domestic price level usually assumed is that illustrated by Cases I, II and III (a).[1] The other cases, although of very much less practical importance, have a decided theoretical interest.

d) *Alterations in the Terms of Trade:* In considering the alterations in the terms of trade produced by an indemnity or loan,

[1] Jacob Viner, *Canada's Balance of International Indebtedness*, pp. 227-37.

we must be careful to distinguish the terms of trade in quantities of commodities from the terms of trade in resources costs.

If $z_{\frac{1}{2}}$ be accepted as an index of the terms of trade in resources costs,[1] i.e., as an index of the ratio of a quantity of country 2's resources to a quantity of country 1's resources, which yield products of equal exchange value, an increase in $z_{\frac{1}{2}}$ would reflect a benefit to country 1 or a detriment to country 2, or indicate both these effects. From the tabulated solutions of the cases in section a it is at once evident that the payment of an indemnity by country 2 to country 1 in cases characterized by stable equilibrium invariably increases $z_{\frac{1}{2}}$, or improves the terms of trade in resources costs for country 1.

The commodity terms of trade, or in Taussig's terminology, the net barter terms of trade, is defined as the ratio of a quantity of representative exports to a quantity of representative imports of equal exchange value. Its variations are conveniently measured by dividing a price index of imports by a price index of exports. Since the barter terms of trade may be regarded as the price paid for imports in exports, any decrease therein is considered favorable and any increase unfavorable.

The reaction of the commodity terms of trade to loans and indemnities has been studied both deductively and inductively. In particular, the arguments advanced by Taussig[2] and the more guarded statements of Viner[3] seek to demonstrate that the receipt of a tribute or a loan improves the commodity terms of trade and that the payment of a tribute or the extension of a loan has the opposite effect. Statistical investigations have also led to results which are frequently in accord with this generalization. It will be interesting to compare this conclusion with those which can be derived from our analysis.

[1] See chapter ii, section 7.

[2] F. W. Taussig, *International Trade*, pp. 114–18.

[3] Jacob Viner, *op. cit.*, pp. 227–37.

In the cases of section a, $\dfrac{y_{11}}{y_{12}}$, $\left(= \dfrac{y_{11}r_1}{y_{12}r_1} = \dfrac{Y_{11}}{Y_{12}} \right)$, would vary proportionately with the commodity terms of trade for country 1 which receives the loan or indemnity. But

$$d\left(\frac{y_{11}}{y_{12}}\right) \gtreqless 0 \qquad \text{as} \qquad \frac{dy_{11}}{y_{11}} \gtreqless \frac{dy_{12}}{y_{12}} . \tag{130}$$

Substituting from (111) and (112), we obtain

$$d\left(\frac{y_{11}}{y_{12}}\right) \gtreqless 0 \quad \text{as} \quad -\frac{+(dI')b_{21}(b_{12}+b_{22})}{\Delta_{11}} \gtreqless -\frac{+(dI')(b_{11}+b_{21})b_{22}}{\Delta_{11}} , \tag{131}$$

or as

$$\frac{b_{21}b_{12}}{\Delta_{11}} \lesseqgtr \frac{b_{11}b_{22}}{\Delta_{11}} ,$$

or as

$$\frac{h_{21}h_{12}}{\Delta_{11}} \lesseqgtr \frac{h_{11}h_{22}}{\Delta_{11}} . \tag{132}$$

If Δ_{11} is positive, this reduces to

$$d\left(\frac{y_{11}}{y_{12}}\right) \gtreqless 0 \qquad \text{as} \qquad h_{21}h_{12} \lesseqgtr h_{11}h_{22} ; \tag{133}$$

but if Δ_{11} is negative, it becomes

$$d\left(\frac{y_{11}}{y_{12}}\right) \gtreqless 0 \qquad \text{as} \qquad h_{21}h_{12} \gtreqless h_{11}h_{22} . \tag{134}$$

For Cases I to III (a), therefore, the commodity terms of trade for the indemnity-receiving country would become better or worse according as the product of the two export supply elasticities was larger or smaller than the product of the two import demand elasticities. And it would seem that the product of the export supply elasticities is rather likely to exceed the product of the import demand elasticities. Our somewhat uncertain basis for this statement is the following: (1) The alternative sources of imports are apt to be more restricted than the possible markets for exports. (2) Elasticities of supply (i.e., the $|e|$'s) probably tend on the average to exceed elasticities of demand (the $|\eta|$'s). On the other hand, if the exports of either country or both countries are produced under constant costs, the commodity terms of trade are necessarily changed in favor of the indemnity-receiving country. And if either or both export supply elasticities are negative, the alteration in favor of the indemnity-receiving country is still further reenforced. These conclusions can be drawn from inspection of Cases IV–XII.

Although the usual statements regarding the effects of tribute or loans on the commodity terms of trade are thus probably correct for the majority of cases, they have a much less adequate foundation in the normal case than is generally supposed.

CHAPTER VI

SUMMARY

In the concluding paragraph of the Introduction the more important contributions of this investigation were very briefly indicated. It is now desirable to elaborate that statement.[1]

The equations descriptive of equilibrium in international trade, which were given in chapter ii, provide the foundation for all the subsequent analysis. The first noteworthy aspect of our treatment is the explicit recognition of assumptions, a phase of theoretical argument too often slighted. But the most important feature of the chapter is the introduction of fixed-height, or deflated, schedules which make it possible to extend the ordinary demand and supply relations to the theory of international trade. Complementary to these schedules is the net monetary factor which forms the connecting link between fixed-height schedule prices in the different countries. By use of these devices it is a simple matter to write the equations for equilibrium in the pure theory of international values and generalize them to include any number of countries and commodities. As a rather obvious corollary of the definition of the net monetary factor, it appears that the purchasing power parity theory is limited to a consideration of "compensated monetary changes," i.e., purely monetary phenomena which involve a reciprocal adjustment of the price levels to the exchange rate. A second corollary of some importance is the distinction between the commodity terms of trade and the terms of trade in resources costs. Attention is given finally to the determination of absolute money prices as well as relative prices at equilibrium.

[1] For a statement of the relation of our analysis to the classical doctrine see the section, "Classical Theory," in Appendix II, "Notes on Other Formulations of International Trade Theory."

Chapter iii is an elaboration of the equilibrium equations. Therein it is shown how the equations may be modified to recognize service items, credit transactions and unilateral payments, duties and bounties, transportation costs, rival and complementary demand and supply, and monopoly. Special interest attaches to the treatment of transportation costs as the most important of the impediments to trade and as a type case of joint demand and complementary supply.

Although they were devised independently by the writer, the curves of import demand and export supply in chapter iv are to be found in much earlier works.[1] In our exposition, however, the elasticities appropriate to these curves are introduced, and the relations between such elasticities and those pertaining to the ordinary demand and supply curves are defined. Marshall's international trade elasticities are also analyzed in terms of the import and export elasticities and in terms of the domestic elasticities. Attention is then devoted to some matters which Marshall neglected to explain, namely, the derivation of his curves and the method of analyzing the effects of duties, bounties, etc., upon them. Our new graphic treatment of equilibrium in international trade is not simple enough to be of much practical importance.

In chapter v and Appendix I a technique for the study of the effects of disturbances to equilibrium is developed. This is applied to the general case involving m countries and n commodities and also more intensively to the two-country, two-commodity case. For the most part the conclusions of this chapter coincide with those of the classical doctrine. But additional light is thrown upon stability of equilibrium, behavior of sectional price levels, and reactions in the terms of trade, measured in commodities and measured in resources costs. It is important to note that by an extension of the technique of analysis the findings of this chapter

[1] Auspitz and Lieben, *Recherches sur la théorie du prix*, pp. 267 ff.; H. Cunynghame, *A Geometrical Political Economy*, chap. x.

are shown to be valid for much more general conditions than those assumed in the preceding chapters.

Some hypothesis as to the general form of the relations between the variables under observation is a necessary preliminary to a quantitative measurement of such relations. Thus, in international trade, before the prices and quantities of imports and exports can be related by statistical reduction of the data, there is needed an algebraic statement of the type of interrelations existing. Although the difficulties in the way of statistical analysis of demand and supply in international trade are very great, the algebraic framework on which such a study may build is indicated by this monograph.

APPENDIX I
SOME MATHEMATICAL THEOREMS
I. TWO THEOREMS IN DETERMINANTS

Lemma I.—$m \geqq 1$. $n \geqq 1$. m and n are integers. ξ_i, η_i, a_{ij}, b_{ij}, $(i = 1, \ldots, m; j = 1, \ldots, n)$, are greater than or equal to zero. But at least one of the ξ_i's or η_j's is not zero, and at least one of the a_{ij}'s or b_{ij}'s in each row is not zero. The determinant $D' =$

$$\begin{vmatrix}
\left(\xi_1 + \sum_{1}^{n} a_{1j}\right) & 0 & \cdots & 0 & a_{11} & a_{12} & \cdots & a_{1n} \\
0 & \left(\xi_2 + \sum_{1}^{n} a_{2j}\right) & \cdots & 0 & a_{21} & a_{22} & \cdots & a_{2n} \\
\cdots & \cdots & \cdots & \cdots & \cdots & \cdots & \cdots & \cdots \\
0 & 0 & \cdots \left(\xi_m + \sum_{1}^{n} a_{mj}\right) & a_{m1} & a_{m2} & \cdots & a_{mn} \\
b_{11} & b_{21} & \cdots & b_{m1} & \left(\eta_1 + \sum_{1}^{m} b_{i1}\right) & 0 & \cdots & 0 \\
b_{12} & b_{22} & \cdots & b_{m2} & 0 & \left(\eta_2 + \sum_{1}^{m} b_{i2}\right) & \cdots & 0 \\
\cdots & \cdots & \cdots & \cdots & \cdots & \cdots & \cdots & \cdots \\
b_{1n} & b_{2n} & \cdots & b_{mn} & 0 & 0 & \cdots \left(\eta_n + \sum_{1}^{m} b\right)
\end{vmatrix}$$

is positive.

Let $k = m+n$. Suppose the result is true of all determinants of this type of order $< k$, i.e., of order $1, 2, \ldots, k-1$. Then it is true for those of order k. For if each column is written as

$$
\begin{vmatrix}
\xi_1 + \sum_1^n a_{1j} & \cdots\cdots\cdots\cdots\cdots\cdots\cdots\cdots \\
0 + 0 & \cdots\cdots\cdots\cdots\cdots\cdots\cdots\cdots \\
\cdots\cdots & \cdots\cdots\cdots\cdots\cdots\cdots\cdots\cdots \\
0 + 0 & \cdots\cdots\cdots\cdots\cdots\cdots\cdots\cdots \\
0 + b_{11} & \cdots\cdots\cdots\cdots\cdots\cdots\cdots\cdots \\
0 + b_{12} & \cdots\cdots\cdots\cdots\cdots\cdots\cdots\cdots \\
\cdots\cdots & \cdots\cdots\cdots\cdots\cdots\cdots\cdots\cdots \\
0 + b_{1n} & \cdots\cdots\cdots\cdots\cdots\cdots\cdots\cdots
\end{vmatrix}
$$

then D' may be split up into the sum of positive multiples of 2^{m+n} determinants of the same type, all of which save one are of order $< k$ and so are positive.[1] The exception is obtained by putting all the ξ's and η's equal to zero. But plainly this determinant is zero, since the sum of the first m columns is equal to the sum of the last n columns.

It is sufficient, therefore, to show that the determinant of order 1 is positive. Every such determinant will be merely a positive ξ or η. Each such order 1 determinant obtained by successively splitting up the original determinant and its resulting parts would have, as multipliers, the product of $(k-1)$ ξ's and η's (see footnote 1) drawn from determinants of orders k to 2.

[1] In order to preserve the D' type of the lower order determinants obtained by splitting up the D' determinant of order k, it is necessary with each loss in order to redefine the ξ's and η's and the Σ terms with which they are associated. In each such lower order determinant the Σ must cover only the terms appearing in the same row of that determinant, and the ξ or η must include all the other terms which appeared in the row of the original determinant of order k but have disappeared in the lower order determinant.

The lemma is therefore proved. Every D' type determinant is positive.

Lemma 2.—The determinant $D'' =$

$$
\begin{vmatrix}
0 & 0 & \cdots & 0 & a_{11} & a_{12} & \cdots & a_{1n} \\
0 & \left(\xi_2 + \sum\limits_{1}^{n} a_{2j}\right) & \cdots & 0 & a_{21} & a_{22} & \cdots & a_{2n} \\
\cdots & \cdots & \cdots & \cdots & \cdots & \cdots & \cdots & \cdots \\
0 & 0 & \cdots & \left(\xi_m + \sum\limits_{1}^{n} a_{mj}\right) & a_{m1} & a_{m2} & \cdots & a_{mn} \\
b_{11} & b_{21} & \cdots & b_{m1} & \left(\eta_1 + \sum\limits_{1}^{m} b_{i1}\right) & 0 & \cdots & 0 \\
b_{12} & b_{22} & \cdots & b_{m2} & 0 & \left(\eta_2 + \sum\limits_{1}^{m} b_{i2}\right) & \cdots & 0 \\
\cdots & \cdots & \cdots & \cdots & \cdots & \cdots & \cdots & \cdots \\
b_{1n} & b_{2n} & \cdots & b_{mn} & 0 & 0 & \cdots & \left(\eta_n + \sum\limits_{1}^{m} b_{in}\right)
\end{vmatrix}
$$

is negative.

This determinant is of order $m+n=k$. Suppose the result were true for all determinants of the type D'' of order $<k$, i.e., $(2, \ldots, k-1)$. Then it can be shown to be true for D'' of order k. As before, we can split up D'' of order k into the sum of positive

multiples of $2^{(m+n-1)}$ determinants, all save one of order $<k$, of type D'', and therefore negative. The exception is of order k and is obtained by putting all the ξ's and η's equal to zero. If for this exception, the columns 2 to m be added to column 1 and the last n columns be subtracted from column 1, the determinant will be

$$
\begin{vmatrix}
\sum_1^n a_{1j} & 0 & \cdots & 0 & a_{11} & a_{12} & \cdots & a_{1n} \\
0 & \left(\xi_2 + \sum_1^n a_{2j}\right) & \cdots & 0 & a_{21} & a_{22} & \cdots & a_{2n} \\
\cdots & \cdots & \cdots & \cdots & \cdots & \cdots & \cdots & \cdots \\
0 & 0 & \cdots & \left(\xi_m + \sum_1^n a_{mj}\right) & a_{m1} & a_{m2} & \cdots & a_{mn} \\
0 & b_{21} & \cdots & b_{m1} & \left(\eta_1 + \sum_1^m b_{i1}\right) & 0 & \cdots & 0 \\
0 & b_{22} & \cdots & b_{m2} & 0 & \left(\eta_2 + \sum_1^m b_{i2}\right) & \cdots & 0 \\
\cdots & \cdots & \cdots & \cdots & \cdots & \cdots & \cdots & \cdots \\
0 & b_{2n} & \cdots & b_{mn} & 0 & 0 & \cdots & \left(\eta_n + \sum_1^m b_{in}\right)
\end{vmatrix}
$$

By expansion this exception becomes $-\sum_{j=1}^{j=n} a_{1j}$ times a minor of type D', which is positive. This exceptional determinant is therefore negative. To prove the lemma, it only remains to show that the lowest order determinant of type D'' is negative. All such determinants of order 1 are zero. The order 2 determinants of type D'' which do not vanish are

$$\begin{vmatrix} 0 & a \\ b & \eta+b \end{vmatrix}$$

and are obviously negative.

Lemma 2 is therefore proved.

2. A THEOREM IN LINEAR EQUATIONS

In the determinant given below, the elements in the rows represent the coefficients of the unknowns in $(m+n-1)$ linear equations. The b's are coefficients of the y's, $(y_2$ to $y_m)$, and the a's are the coefficients of the x's, $(x_1$ to $x_n)$ (see footnote 1). The k's are the constants on the right-hand side of the equations and are assumed to be all of the same sign. The a's and b's are $\geqq 0$, but at least one of the a's or b's in each row does not vanish.

[1] The x's and y's are used here as general symbols for unknowns. For purposes of chapter V the x of the Appendix corresponds to $\dfrac{dy_{1i}}{y_{1i}}$ of the text, and y to $\dfrac{dz_1}{z_1}$.

$$
\left|
\begin{array}{cccccccc}
a_{2i} & 0 & \cdots & 0 & a_{21} & a_{22} & \cdots & a_{2n} \\
0 & \sum_1^n a_{3i} & \cdots & 0 & a_{31} & a_{32} & \cdots & a_{3n} \\
\cdots & \cdots & \cdots & \cdots & \cdots & \cdots & \cdots & \cdots \\
0 & 0 & \cdots & \sum_1^n a_{mi} & a_{m1} & a_{m2} & \cdots & a_{mn} \\
b_{21} & b_{31} & \cdots & b_{m1} & \left(b_{11}+\sum_2^m b_{i1}\right) & 0 & \cdots & 0 \\
b_{22} & b_{32} & \cdots & b_{m2} & 0 & \left(b_{12}+\sum_2^m b_{i2}\right) & \cdots & 0 \\
\cdots & \cdots & \cdots & \cdots & \cdots & \cdots & \cdots & \cdots \\
b_{2n} & b_{3n} & \cdots & b_{mn} & 0 & 0 & \cdots & \left(b_{1n}+\sum_2^m b_{in}\right)
\end{array}
\right|
\begin{array}{c}
k_2 \\ k_3 \\ \cdots \\ k_m \\ 0 \\ 0 \\ \cdots \\ 0
\end{array}
$$

From the last n equations it is evident that if all the y's are of the same sign, the x's are all of the opposite sign. It is necessary, therefore, only to show that all the y's are of the same sign, which is the sign of the k's. Let us call the determinant above Δ_{11} since the rows and columns are both numbered beginning with 2.

Obviously, Δ_{11} is of the type D' and positive. The minor, $\Delta_{11,22}$, is also of type D' and positive. $\Delta_{11,23}$ is, however, of type D'' and therefore negative. The minor, $\Delta_{11,24}$, is, after one interchange of rows, of type D'' and therefore has the sign $-(-)$ or positive.

The minor, $\Delta_{11,25}$, is, after two interchanges of rows, of type D'' and therefore negative. Thus the minors alternate in sign and, in general $\Delta_{11,2q}$, $(q \leqq m)$, has the sign $-(-1)^{q-3}$ or $(-1)^q$.

Now

$$y_2 = \frac{k_2 \Delta_{11,\ 22} - k_3 \Delta_{11,\ 23} + k_4 \Delta_{11,\ 24} - \cdots + k_m(-1)^m \Delta_{11,\ 2m}}{\Delta_{11}}.$$

But since the $\Delta_{11,2q}$'s alternate in sign, beginning with a positive, it follows that the numerator is of the same sign as the sign of the k's (which is assumed to be uniform). Since Δ_{11} has been shown positive, y_2 is therefore of the same sign as the k's. But every y, (y_2 to y_m), is consequently of the sign of the k's, for it is quite immaterial which of the y's is y_2, and any other y may be interchanged in position with y_2 by simply shifting an even number of rows and columns.

It should be noticed that the demonstration is unaffected if some, not all, of the k's are equal to zero.

Thus we have shown (a) that all the y's, (y_2 to y_m), have the same sign, which is the uniform sign of the k's, and (b) that all the x's, (x_1 to x_n), have the opposite sign from that of the k's.

APPENDIX II

NOTES ON OTHER FORMULATIONS OF INTER-NATIONAL TRADE THEORY

Classical Theory

As was pointed out in chapter i, this monograph is merely a mathematical exposition and development of the classical theory of international trade. Classical theory in its later stages incorporated, *inter alia*, the following concepts: various forms of the quantity theory of money; demand and supply schedules or functions (although these were not used definitely in international trade theory, but instead the rather vague term "reciprocal demand"); the uniformity of competitive prices of internationally traded commodities, with allowances for barriers; J. S. Mill's "Equation of International Demand," stipulating the equality of the values of exports and imports for a country; and the maintenance of this equality through the shifts of price levels, brought about by changes in the quantity of money in circulation in the various countries or by changes in the exchange rates. These concepts find expression in our equations.

Certain other concepts and methods of approach employed by the classical school are much less prominent or are omitted in our treatment. The most striking contrast appears in our use of "deflated" money supply schedules instead of labor or real sacrifice costs. Although the doctrine of comparative costs is not explicitly recognized in our equilibrium equations, it is obvious that it could readily be stated in terms of relative supply prices. For this purpose the fixed-schedule or deflated prices, i.e., the y_{pk}'s, may be used. Or, if the ratio of the supply prices of the two commodities in one country be compared with the corresponding ratio in the other country, the actual money supply prices may be utilized.

An exposition of the theory of comparative costs in terms of supply prices instead of real costs was given by Pareto[1] in his early writings and, less satisfactorily, by J. S. Nicholson in his *Principles of Political Economy*. Professor Taussig, subsequent to the publication of his book, *International Trade*, indicated to the writer the desirability of approaching the problem in this way and then moving on to a discussion in terms of sacrifice costs.

The advantages of using prices instead of sacrifice costs and utilities in approaching the theory of international trade are readily appreciated. If the price and quantity phenomena are dealt with by a simple extension of the ordinary treatment of supply and demand, the difficulties of defining sacrifice costs and relating them to money costs do not confuse the introductory analysis. Then, after the price-quantity interactions have been adequately described, the subjective elements may be taken into consideration. On the other hand, an introduction to the theory of international trade in terms of sacrifice costs or in terms of costs measured in quantities of productive factors does avoid some difficulties arising out of shifting price levels. But the perplexing relations between real costs and money costs must then be considered immediately or some simplifying assumption must be made. Furthermore, this approach has not led to a clear and accurate description of the immediately observable price-quantity phenomena.

Although the analysis of the theory of international trade in this monograph has been almost entirely related to such observable phenomena, it is, of course, true that the really important elements in any economic situation are subjective. Thus, while Angell's argument for an analysis in terms of prices is well taken,[2] his unwillingness to plumb beneath them is ill considered.[3] Still,

---

[1] "Teoria matematica del commercio internazionale," *Giornale degli Economisti*, X (1895), 476–98; *Cours d'économie politique*, pp. 209 ff.; *Manuel d'économie politique*, pp. 505 ff.

[2] J. W. Angell, *The Theory of International Prices*, pp. 461 ff.

[3] Jacob Viner, "Angell's 'Theory of International Prices,' " *Journal of Political Economy*, XXXIV (1926), 622–23.

the outright refusal to deal with the transition from prices to human values is less dangerous than the failure to appreciate the difficulties involved. The classical economists were, in general, too prone to assume the proportionality of the quantity of labor or of composite resources expended to sacrifice cost and to money cost, respectively.

Without any pretense at tracing the history of the theory of international trade, we shall note briefly the principal contributions to which our algebraic and graphic methods are related.

Alfred Marshall

Among the major accomplishments of Marshall in the theory of international trade were his invention and application of a graphic technique. The curves of international exchange, the concepts of elasticities referring to these curves, the identification of stable and unstable equilibria, and the elaborate analysis of disturbances and their effects upon the terms of trade are the features of his work of greatest interest to us. The relation of our treatment to Marshall's methods was set forth at some length in chapter iv, sections 4–6, and we need not repeat it here.

F. Y. Edgeworth

In his series of articles on "The Theory of International Values" in the *Economic Journal*,[1] Edgeworth made illuminating criticisms on the contributions of other writers. The constructive portions of his papers were devoted to a graphic analysis of a variety of problems and an algebraic description of equilibrium.

In the course of an otherwise brilliant application of the Marshallian graphics, he fell into a curious error. While discussing the effects of taxes and other impediments to imports or exports,[2] he affirmed that, whereas a tax or impediment to exports always shortens the export co-ordinate (in Figure 11, the abscissa

---

[1] *Op. cit.*, IV (1894), 35–50, 424–43, 606–38. Reproduced with some modifications as "The Pure Theory of International Values" in Edgeworth's *Papers Relating to Political Economy*, II, 3–60.

[2] *Economic Journal*, IV (1894), 429–35.

of OE), a tax or impediment to imports always *lengthens the import co-ordinate* of the curve (the ordinate of OE). This asymmetry and its consequences he regarded as the most distinctive contribution of the mathematical method. As was shown in chapter iv, section 5, an impediment to imports also *shortens the export co-ordinate* of the Marshallian curve.

Although the effects of import duties and export duties on the Marshallian curve, and therefore on the commodity terms of trade, are symmetrical, other results of these disturbances are unlike. In the latter part of section 3, chapter v, it was shown that an import duty levied by country 1 raises the height of its schedules and hence its domestic price level relative to those of country 2 (z_3 increases). It was also pointed out that an export duty would have these same effects if the foreign demand for the imports of country 1 were inelastic. But if, as is more likely, the foreign demand is elastic, the results would be reversed: the schedules and domestic price level of country 1 would fall relative to those of country 2.

Edgeworth's algebraic description of equilibrium starts with composite utility functions for each of the two countries and a constant amount of work (measured in disutility) expended in each country on the production of internationally traded commodities. The utility function for each country is then maximized, subject to the conditions of constant costs of production, fixed quantity of resources, and the equality of values of imports and exports. Edgeworth's equations are adequate to indicate the status at equilibrium; but in his illustration, at least, they are limited to constant costs and are not as closely related as are our equations to the demand and supply functions and the prices with which economists are most familiar. They involve, moreover, the vague and questionable concept of utility or disutility for a country as a whole.

In passing, we should call attention to Edgeworth's symbol v, "the number of units of work in the first country, of which the product is equivalent in value to the product of a unit of work in the second country." If the disutility of production, in Edgeworth's sense, were proportional to the deflated supply price, y_{pk}, in each country, this v would be proportional to the reciprocal of our $z_{\frac{1}{2}}$.

H. Cunynghame

The curves of import demand and export supply, together with their derivation from the ordinary domestic demand and supply

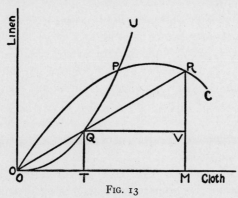

FIG. 13

curves, are to be found in Cunynghame's *A Geometrical Political Economy*, chapter x. But the analysis of the "exceptional" case of import demand when the domestic supply curve for the commodity would be negatively sloped is not differentiated from that for the ordinary case. Consequently, the author is led into a somewhat fantastic explanation of equilibrium for the exceptional case.[1]

Cunynghame's attempt to explain the derivation of Marshall's curves is confused and erroneous. In Figure 13, a reproduction of Figure 56 in *A Geometrical Political Economy*, *OU* is the locus of a point whose co-ordinates are quantities of cloth and linen having equal total effective utilities, and *OC* is the locus of a point whose co-ordinates are quantities of cloth and linen having equal total

[1] *A Geometrical Political Economy*, pp. 87–89.

costs of production.[1] As regards exclusively domestic trade, the co-ordinates of P would indicate the quantities of cloth and linen produced and exchanged against each other. But the problem is more complex if a portion of one commodity is exported and a portion of the other commodity is imported. If OM cloth were produced, its total cost would be equal to that of MR linen. And since OT and TQ bear, respectively, the same proportion to OM and MR, it would be true that OT cloth and TQ linen would have equal costs of production *assuming the scale of output of cloth to be OM and the scale of output of linen to be MR*. Further, OT cloth and TQ linen would have equal total effective utilities *if they were the whole quantities on the market*. But it does not follow that, when the scale of output of cloth is OM, the portion OT of cloth would exchange for the whole domestic production TQ of linen, leaving TM (or QV) cloth to be exported for VR linen. For this violates the two italicized assumptions. The scale of production of linen is no longer MR but TQ, and the quantity of linen on the market is no longer TQ but MR. Consequently, QV and VR cannot be taken to represent the co-ordinates of a point on a Marshallian international trade curve of demand for linen in terms of cloth. The attempt to derive a Marshallian curve of import of cloth and export of linen from Figure 13 by a similar procedure would likewise fail. These procedures which would be correct (though not applicable in this problem) if the ordinates were total money value or cost fail when the ordinates are quantities of second commodity of varying value and cost of production. It is not difficult to understand that Marshall should have raised objections to Cunyghame's interpretations of his curves.

J. W. Angell

In the last chapter of his *Theory of International Prices* Angell obtained some novel effects with the Marshallian curves. Al-

---

[1] Cunynghame's definition of these curves is not at all clear. This seemed the most reasonable interpretation of his statements.

though the exposition is not easy to interpret, it would seem that each Marshallian curve is to be constructed out of the demand and supply curves of each country on the assumption of perfect competition. But since competition often is not keen, producers and traders frequently get something more than a competitive return. In such cases the point whose co-ordinates indicate the quantities exchanged lies somewhere within the area bounded by the curves. This treatment, however, neglects the opposite cases of excessive competition in which producers cannot recoup their costs because of a decline in demand or an overexpansion of the industry.

Aside from the effects of imperfect competition, Angell's arguments on the indeterminateness of the terms of trade are not impressive. The treatment of transportation costs is quite unsatisfactory. If the conditions of supply and demand for transportation services are competitive and are known, they do not bring into the situation an indeterminate element, as we have demonstrated in chapter iii, section 5, and suggested in chapter iv, section 5.

Nor is Angell's analysis of the multi-commodity barter case valid. Surely the assumption that barter reduces to a "series of pairs of independent operations" is a gratuitous and unreasonable assumption. On the contrary, we should expect the most intimate relations between the barter exchanges of different commodities as traders sought out the best bargains. Further, the important balance of values would not be that of the individual transactions but that for the whole value of imports and exports of a country. This is the only reasonable sense in which Mill's "Equation of International Demand" is to be interpreted.

As regards the effects of money on the terms of trade, Angell points out that dynamic monetary changes are particularly important in the short run and leave their impress more or less permanently on an economic system.

A. A. Cournot

Cournot's most important contributions appeared in his first book, *Researches into the Mathematical Principles of the Theory of Wealth*. But they relate to a single commodity which forms so small a portion of the total value of imports or exports that the repercussions of disturbances upon price levels may be neglected. We shall not stop to review Cournot's conclusions since they fall outside the scope of the general theory of international trade.

We are, however, indebted to Cournot for his independent development of demand and supply functions and for his use of the Taylor expansion in studying the effects of small disturbances upon an equilibrium situation.

Leon Walras

The name of Leon Walras is included here, not because of any direct contributions to the theory of international trade, but because of his development of the algebraic description of equilibrium for a single country. The two sets of equations (Sets I and II) which are the basis of our exposition are analogous, respectively, to those which express the equality of the values of sales and purchases for each individual and to those which express the equality of the sum of the quantities of a commodity sold to the sum of the quantities bought.

Auspitz and Lieben

Auspitz and Lieben derived and used curves of import demand and export supply in total form. But, since they consistently adopted total *money* value or cost as ordinates, their curves are to be distinguished from Marshall's curves of international exchange.

Their conclusions, like Cournot's, are applicable to a single commodity which forms so small a portion of the total value of imports and exports that the effects on price levels may be neglected.

Vilfred Pareto

The most pretentious mathematical analysis of the theory of international trade known to the writer is that by Vilfred Pareto.[1] In abbreviated form his procedure is as follows: The equations describing the economic system of two countries as separate entities are first written. If these countries now engage in international trade, i.e., import and export certain products (but not productive services), new unknowns are introduced. These are the n quantities of the n commodities exchanged between the two markets and the rate of exchange between the money units of the two countries—in all $(n+1)$ unknowns. But there are $(n+1)$ additional equations. The value of exports is equal to the value of imports (one equation serves for either country). And n equations state that the prices of the n international commodities are equivalent in the two countries, allowing for the (known) costs of surmounting any barriers to trade.

This treatment seems extraordinarily simple. It does not involve explicitly the quantity theory of money or make any reference to shifting price levels in the respective countries. How, then, can the equations be adequate to describe equilibrium in international trade?

Among the imports or exports of each country there ordinarily appears the commodity gold. When equilibrium is achieved, it must be true, for gold as for other commodities, that the demand in the two countries combined is equal to the supply. If the two countries are on the gold standard, the equilibrium which is reached after any disturbance (such as an indemnity) is introduced, would be characterized by *domestic* prices which had shifted in response to changes in the utility of gold and in its cost

---

[1] An extensive treatment appears in his two articles in the *Giornale degli Economisti:* "Teoria matematica dei cambi forestieri," VIII (1894), 142–73; and "Teoria matematica del commercio internazionale," X (1895), 476–98. Much of this is reproduced in the *Cours d'économie politique.* In the *Manuel d'économie politique* the general mathematical analysis is much abbreviated.

of production and by prices *of internationally traded commodities* which had altered in response to these changes for gold and also because the quantities of these commodities produced and consumed had changed. The equilibrium depicted is analogous to that which is obtained in chapter ii, section 9, when the demand for and supply of gold for all countries combined is stipulated in the equations.

Such an equilibrium, as we have said, is approached but very slowly. It would be highly desirable to be able to consider the incomplete equilibrium which is more quickly achieved through a redistribution of the gold stock of the world, even though the demand for gold in the arts plus the demand to maintain the monetary stock were not exactly equated to the supply. This could be done approximately in Pareto's equations, as in ours, by omitting the commodity gold or by assuming the value of gold imports and exports to be known. The use of an ordinary commodity as a *numéraire* in Pareto's system would not involve any inconvenience. But in any case, Pareto's equations do not explicitly recognize—in fact, they mask rather effectively—the shifts of price levels which are so prominent in the classical theory. It is interesting to observe that in the context of these equations the discussion of disturbances to equilibrium devotes considerable attention to the quantity theory of money and shifts of price levels and rather neglects the long-run adjustment of prices to the utility and cost of production of gold as required in the algebraic exposition.

In summary, the major points which distinguish Pareto's equations from ours are the following:

1. The former involve the utility functions of individuals, the factors of production, and, in fact, all the elements in Pareto's description of internal equilibrium.

2. They are limited to two countries, but they could be extended to the general case.

3. They are not clearly related to monetary mechanisms and shifts in price levels.

4. The effects of disturbances to equilibrium cannot, through them, be readily associated with particular elasticities of demand and supply.

5. If all the equations of both countries are included, the system is very much more complicated than ours and less amenable to the analysis of the effects of disturbances to equilibrium.

There are other features of Pareto's treatment which should be noted. It includes a demonstration that the Marshallian curves may be derived from his equations by the elimination of all the unknowns except the quantities of the two commodities respectively imported and exported. In order to investigate the effects of disturbances, Pareto used small finite differences; but his procedure was much less general and systematic than ours. He also developed a somewhat complicated measure of the gain or loss resulting from disturbances to international trade. Not least significant of his accomplishments, though among the simplest from a mathematical viewpoint, was his exposition of the theory of comparative costs in terms of relative prices. It is unfortunate that this treatment suffered from a needless complexity of symbols.

We cannot help deploring that the unfinished treatise on international trade for which Pareto is reported to have accumulated extensive notes should never have reached fruition.

Pietri-Tonelli

This writer has taken Pareto's contributions and expounded them with added clarity.

BIBLIOGRAPHY[1]

ANGELL, JAMES W. *The Theory of International Prices*. Cambridge, 1926.

AUSPITZ, RUDOLF, and LIEBEN, RICHARD. *Recherches sur la théorie du prix*. Translated from the German by Louis Suret. Paris, 1914. German edition, Leipzig, 1889.

CAIRNES, J. E. *Some Leading Principles of Political Economy*. London, 1874.

COURNOT, A. A. *Researches into the Mathematical Principles of the Theory of Wealth*. Translated by N. T. Bacon. New York, 1927. Original French edition, Paris, 1838.

CUNYNGHAME, H. *A Geometrical Political Economy*. Oxford, 1904.

EDGEWORTH, F. Y. "The Theory of International Values," *Economic Journal*, IV (1894), 35-50, 424-43, 606-38. Reprinted with some modifications in his *Papers Relating to Political Economy*, II, 3-60. London, 1925.

MARSHALL, ALFRED. *The Pure Theory of Foreign Trade*. Privately printed, 1879. Reprinted together with *The Pure Theory of Domestic Values*. London, 1930.

————. *Money, Credit and Commerce*. London, 1923.

MILL, JOHN STUART. *Principles of Political Economy*. London, 1848.

NICHOLSON, J. S. *Principles of Political Economy*. 3 vols. London, 1893-1901.

OHLIN, BERTIL. *The Reparations Problem*, Index, No. 28 (April, 1928). Svenska Handelsbanken, Stockholm.

PANTALEONI, MAFFEO. *Pure Economics*. Translated by T. B. Bruce. London, 1913. Original Italian edition, Florence, 1889.

PARETO, VILFRED. "Teoria matematica dei cambi forestieri," *Giornale degli Economisti*, VIII (1894), 142-73.

————. "Teoria matematica del commercio internazionale," *ibid.*, X (1895), 476-98.

————. *Cours d'économie politique*. Lausanne, 1896-97.

————. *Manuel d'économie politique*. Translated by Alfred Bonnet. Paris, 1909. Original Italian edition, Milan, 1906.

PIETRI-TONELLI, ALFONSO DE. *Traité d'économie rationelle*. Paris, 1927.

PIGOU, A. C., and ROBERTSON, D. H. *Economic Essays and Addresses*. London, 1931. Part I, chap. iv and Part II, chap. iv.

[1] For a more extensive bibliography on the theory of international trade the reader is referred to J. W. Angell, *The Theory of International Prices*, pp. 535-56.

RICARDO, DAVID. *Principles of Political Economy and Taxation.* E. C. K. Gonner's edition. London, 1891. Original edition, London, 1817.

TAUSSIG, F. W. *International Trade.* New York, 1927.

VINER, JACOB. *Canada's Balance of International Indebtedness, 1900–1913.* Cambridge, 1924.

WALRAS, LEON. *Éléments d'économie politique pure.* Lausanne, 1874.

WHEWELL, W. "Mathematical Exposition of Some of the Leading Doctrines in Mr. Ricardo's 'Principles of Political Economy.'" *Transactions of the Cambridge Philosophical Society, IV* (1833), 155–98.

———. "Mathematical Exposition of Some Doctrines of Political Economy," *ibid.,* IX (1856), Part I, 128–49.

———. "Mathematical Exposition of Certain Doctrines of Political Economy," *ibid.,* IX (1856), Part II, 1–7.

YNTEMA, T. O. "The Influence of Dumping on Monopoly Price," *Journal of Political Economy,* XXXVI (1928), 686–98.

GLOSSARY OF SYMBOLS

This glossary includes only symbols which are used outside the immediate context of their definition.

Subscripts

d—Refers to demand; always followed by a comma.
s—Refers to supply; always followed by a comma.
First subscript (or first after a comma) denotes the country.
Second subscript (or second after a comma) denotes the commodity.
p—General subscript for a country.
k—General subscript for a commodity.
i—General subscript in summations.

Quantities of Commodities

$q_{d,pk}$—Quantity demanded.
$q_{s,pk}$—Quantity supplied.
x_{pk}—Quantity exported $(+)$ or imported $(-)$.

Prices of Commodities

Y_{pk}—Actual money price.
y_{pk}—Deflated or fixed-height schedule price.

Functional Relations between Prices and Quantities

$$q_{d,pk} = \psi_{d,pk}(y_{pk}) \ .$$

$$q_{s,pk} = \psi_{s,pk}(y_{pk}) \ .$$

$$x_{pk} = f_{pk}(y_{pk}) \ .$$

$$y_{pk} = \phi_{pk}(x_{pk}) \ .$$

Exchange Rate

$c_{\frac{1}{p}}$—The number of units of country p's currency obtainable for one unit of the currency of country 1.

Index of Height of Actual Money Schedules

$r_p = \dfrac{Y_{pk}}{y_{pk}}$, i.e., the ratio for country p of the height of its actual demand and supply schedules to the height of its fixed-height or deflated schedules.

Net Monetary Factor

$z_{\frac{1}{p}} = c_1 \dfrac{r_1}{r_p} = \dfrac{y_{pk}}{y_{1k}}$. If barriers exist, $z_{\frac{1}{p}}$ is equal to the ratio of y_{pk} to y_{1k} after either is appropriately modified to compensate for the barriers.

Elasticities

e_{pk}—Elasticity of supply.

η_{pk}—Elasticity of demand.

h_{pk}—Elasticity of export supply or import demand.

$h_{s,pk}$—Elasticity of export supply.

$h_{d,pk}$—Elasticity of import demand.

$E_{d,p\frac{k}{k'}}$—Marshall's elasticity of demand for his curves, i.e., the elasticity of the demand of country p for its imports, k, in terms of its exports, k'.

Other symbols

T—An ad valorem duty.

T'—A specific duty.

B'—A specific bounty.

$I_{(p \leftarrow p')}$—An indemnity payable by country p' to country p, measured in the currency of country p.

$a_{pk} = x_{pk}y_{pk}(1 + h_{pk})$.

$b_{pk} = x_{pk}h_{pk}$.

Δ_{11}—A determinant of the type (99) in chapter v, section 2.

INDEX

Angell, James W., 104, 108–9, 114

Assumptions:
  ceteris paribus assumption, 1, 2
  relaxation of, 26–40, 73–78
  statement of, 4–7

Auspitz, Rudolph, 41 n., 94 n., 110, 114

Bounties, 26, 30–31, 45–47, 50–52, 72–73. *See also* Equilibrium, disturbances to

Bowley, A. L., 7–8 n.

Cairnes, J. E., 114

Classical theory of international trade, 1, 2, 103–5

Commodities, subscript symbols, 7

Comparative costs, 103–4, 113

Constant monetary conditions. *See* Monetary conditions, constant

Countries:
  definition of, 3
  subscript symbols, 7

Cournot, A. A., 63 n., 110, 114

Credit transactions, 27–29, 50–52. *See also* Equilibrium, disturbances to

Cunynghame, H., 41 n., 94 n., 107–8, 114

Demand and supply:
  assumption of demand and supply schedules, 5–7
  effects of impediments on import demand and export supply, 45–47
  fixed-height schedules, 8–10
  generalization of demand and supply functions, 37–38
  import demand and export supply, 8–9, 41–43
  reciprocal demand, 2
  symbols, 8–9
  See also Elasticities, Duties, Bounties, Impediments, Transportation costs

Determinants, theorems in, 96–100

Duties, 26, 29–30, 45–47, 50–52, 72–73. *See also* Equilibrium, disturbances to

Dynamic monetary changes. *See* Monetary changes

Edgeworth, F. Y., 52 n., 105–7, 114

Elasticities:
  domestic demand and supply, 43–45
  import demand and export supply, 43–45
  Marshall's international trade curves, 52–56

Equilibrium:
  conditions of, 4, 7, 12
  Disturbances to:
    dynamic character of, 38–39
    effects of disturbances in general case, 68–71, 77–78
    effects of disturbances in two-country, two-commodity cases, 80–90
    shifts of schedules and price points, 12, 61–62
    technique of analyzing effect of disturbances, 63–68, 73–78, 78–79, 96–102, 113
  equations describing, 12–17, 21–22, 23–25, 26–40, 111–13
  graphic solutions:
    Marshall's, 47–50
    a new solution, 56–58
  stability of, 59, 79–80, 87

Exchange, fundamental character of, 4

Exchange rate, 10, 18. *See also* Equilibrium equations

Fisher, Irving, 63 n.

Fixed-height schedules. *See* Demand and supply

Gold, 23–25

Graphic methods, 41–60, 105–6, 107–8, 109, 110, 113

Impediments to trade, 29–31, 45–47. *See also* Duties, Bounties, *and* Transportation costs

Indemnities, 27–29, 50–52. *See also* Equilibrium, disturbances to

PRINTED
IN U·S·A

Materials for the Study of Business

Edited by WILLIAM H. SPENCER

TEXTS AND READINGS

THE PHYSICAL ENVIRONMENT OF BUSINESS

An Introduction to Economic Geography. Vol. I. By WELLINGTON D. JONES and DERWENT S. WHITTLESEY. *603 pages, $5.00.*

THE SOCIAL ENVIRONMENT AND SOCIAL CONTROL

Readings in Industrial Society. By L. C. MARSHALL. (Briefer Edition.) *1,082 pages, $4.50.*

Industrial Society. By L. C. MARSHALL. (Revised and Enlarged Edition.) Part I. The Emergence of the Modern Order. *$2.50.* Part II. Production in the Modern Order. *$3.50.* Part III. The Co-ordination of Specialists through the Market. *$4.00.*

Outlines of the Economic Order: Developed in a Series of Problems. By LEON C. MARSHALL, J. F. CHRIST, A. W. KORNHAUSER, L. W. MINTS, and S. H. NERLOVE. *$2.00.*

Social Control of Business. By J. MAURICE CLARK. *500 pages, $4.00.*

Law and Business. By WILLIAM H. SPENCER. Vol. I. Introduction. *612 pages.* Vol. II. Law and the Market. Law and Finance. *670 pages.* Vol. III. Law and Labor. Law and Risk-Bearing. Law and the Form of the Business Unit. *654 pages. Each $4.50.*

A Textbook of Law and Business. By WILLIAM H. SPENCER. *1,116 pages, $5.00.*

FINANCIAL ORGANIZATION AND FINANCIAL ADMINISTRATION

The Financial Organization of Society. By H. G. MOULTON. (Revised Edition, 1930.) *752 pages, $4.00.*

THE WORKER AND PERSONNEL ADMINISTRATION

The Worker in Modern Economic Society. By PAUL H. DOUGLAS, CURTICE N. HITCHCOCK, and WILLARD E. ATKINS. *936 pages, $4.50.*

RISK AND RISK-BEARING

Risk and Risk-Bearing. By CHARLES O. HARDY. (Revised Edition, 1931.) *400 pages, $3.50.*

Readings in Risk and Risk-Bearing. By CHARLES O. HARDY. *368 pages, $3.50.*

BUSINESS ADMINISTRATION AND CONTROL

Managerial Accounting. Vol. I. By J. O. McKINSEY. *655 pages, $4.00.*

Production Management. By W. N. MITCHELL. *444 pages, $4.00.*

Retail Accounting and Control. By A. C. HODGE. *545 pages, $4.00.*

Accounting Method. By C. RUFUS ROREM. (Revised Edition, 1930.) *528 pages, $4.50.*

Teacher's Manual for Accounting Method. By W. J. GRAHAM and C. RUFUS ROREM. *$3.00.*

Business Administration. By L. C. MARSHALL. *919 pages, $4.00.*

THE BUSINESS CURRICULUM

Education for Business. By LEVERETT S. LYON. (Revised Edition, 1931.) *588 pages, $3.50.*

SPECIAL STUDIES

Social Studies in Secondary Schools. By A COMMISSION OF THE ASSOCIATION OF THE COLLEGIATE SCHOOLS OF BUSINESS. *114 pages, $1.00.*

Wages and the Family. By PAUL H. DOUGLAS. (Revised Edition.) *304 pages, $3.00.*

Psychological Tests in Business. By A. W. KORNHAUSER and F. A. KINGSBURY. *194 pages, $1.90.*

The Cold-Storage Industry in the United States. By EDWARD A. DUDDY. *$2.00.*

How to Study. By A. W. KORNHAUSER. *43 pages, 25 cents.*

Business Cases and Problems. By L. C. MARSHALL and others. *363 pages, $3.00.*

Farmers' Mutual Fire Insurance in the United States. By VICTOR N. VALGREN. *200 pages, $1.90.*

The Uses of Bank Funds. By WALDO F. MITCHELL. *181 pages, $2.00.*

The Legal Aspects of Zoning. By NEWMAN F. BAKER. *182 pages, $2.50.*

The Collegiate School of Business. By L. C. MARSHALL and others. *$4.00.*

Efficiency and Scarcity Profits. By C. J. FOREMAN. *$4.00.*

Alfred Weber's Theory of the Location of Industries. Translated and edited by CARL J. FRIEDRICH. *$3.00.*

A Mathematical Reformulation of the General Theory of International Trade. By THEODORE O. YNTEMA. *$2.50.*

THE UNIVERSITY OF CHICAGO PRESS